All About Dogs
FUN-SCHOOLING
JOURNAL
Do-It-Yourself Homeschooling
Curriculum Handbook - 365 Pages

Learning
Ages 7+

THE THINKING TREE

Published By:
THE THINKING TREE, LLC

Created By:
Sarah Janisse Brown & Melissa Knorr

Illustrations:
Anna Kidalova (Dog Breeds and Careers)
Naomi Brown (Digital Art)
Lauren Crowther (Detailed Pencil Drawings)
Melissa Knorr (Comics & Cartoons)
Alexandra Bretush (Mazes)
Photography (Shutterstock)

Copyright 2018— Do Not Copy— Except for Family Use

FUNSCHOOLINGBOOKS.COM

ALL ABOUT DOGS

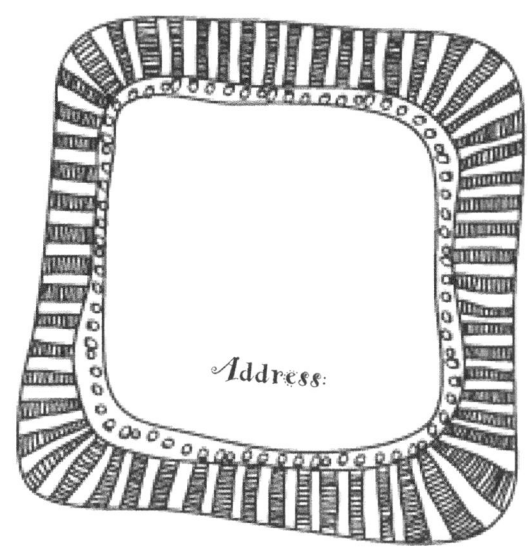

Address:

Name & Age:

Phone & Email:

This Curriculum Covers:

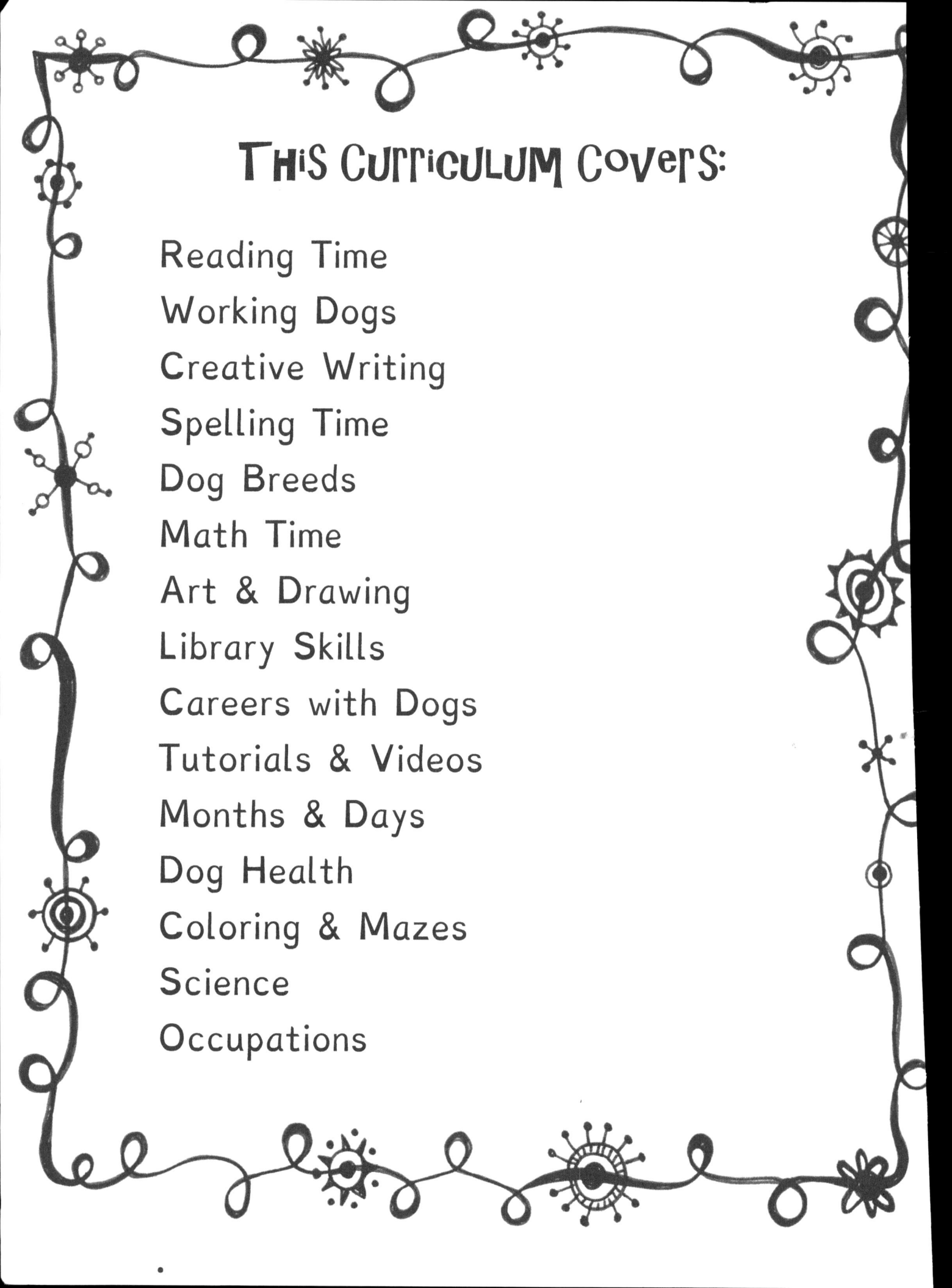

- Reading Time
- Working Dogs
- Creative Writing
- Spelling Time
- Dog Breeds
- Math Time
- Art & Drawing
- Library Skills
- Careers with Dogs
- Tutorials & Videos
- Months & Days
- Dog Health
- Coloring & Mazes
- Science
- Occupations

INSTRUCTIONS

What do you want to know about Dogs?
Make a List, and get books on each topic!

1. 5.
2. 6.
3. 7.
4. 8.

Action Steps:

1. Go to the library or bookstore.
2. Bring home a stack of at least EIGHT interesting books about these topics. Choose some that have diagrams, instructions, historical information about dogs, scientific information about dogs, and illustrations.

Supplies Needed:
You will need pencils, colored pencils, pens, markers and a new set of smooth black drawing pens for picture study and art exercises.

Choose Eight Books To Use As School Books!

1. Write down the titles on each cover below.
2. Keep your stack of books in a safe place.
3. Be ready to read a few pages from your books daily.
4. Complete 10 pages each day in this workbook.

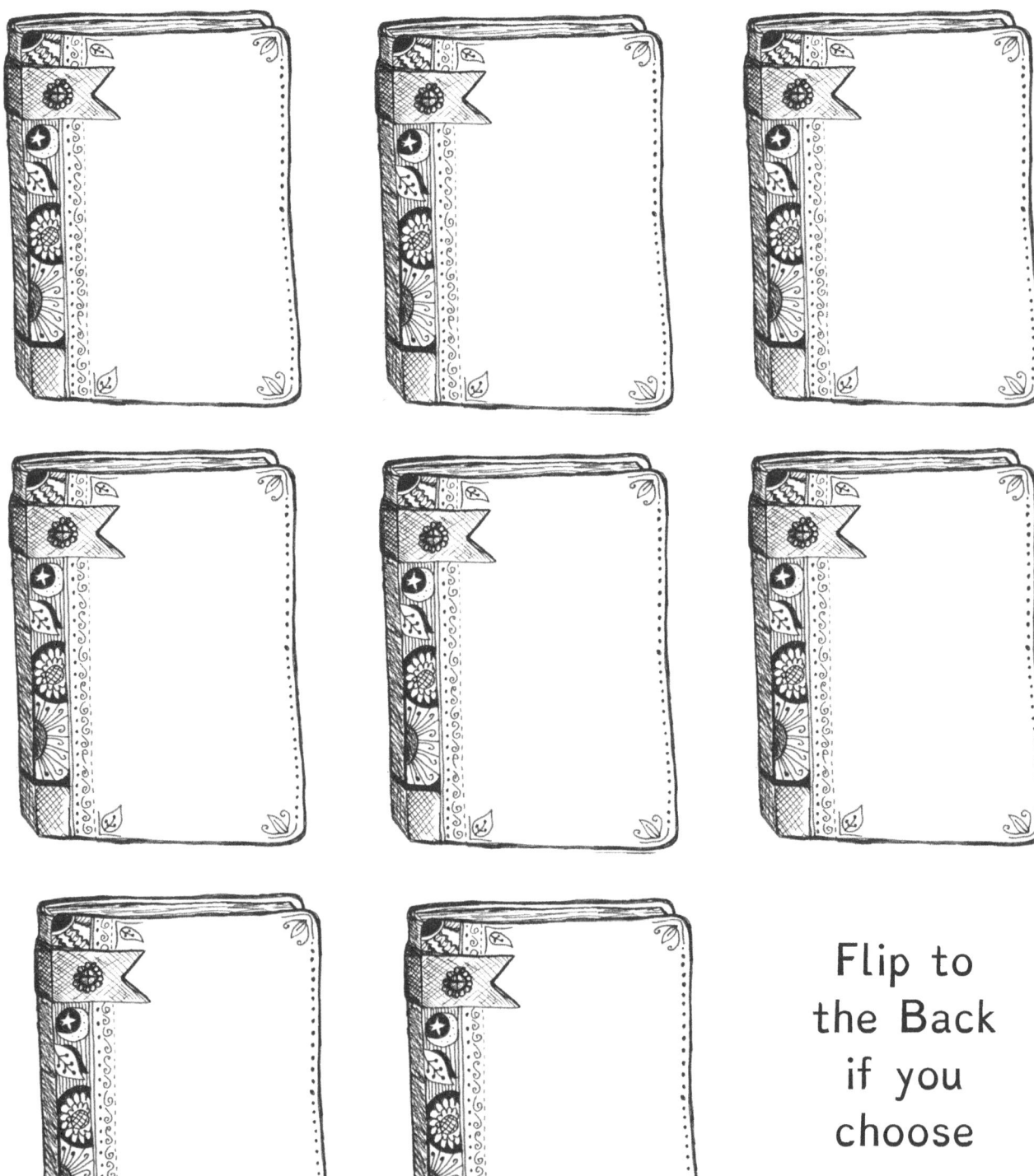

Flip to the Back if you choose more books!

CIRCLE TODAY'S DATE

January
February
March
April
May
June
July
August
September
October
November
December

1 2 3 4 5 6
7 8 9 10 11
12 13 14 15
16 17 18 19
20 21 22 23
24 25 26 27
28 29 30 31

MONDAY
TUESDAY
WEDNESDAY
THURSDAY
FRIDAY
SATURDAY
SUNDAY

2015
2016
2017
2018
2019
2020
2021
2022
2023
2024
2025
2026
2027
2028
2029

Write Today's Date: _ _ _ _ _ _ _ _ _ _ _ _ _

START YOUR DAY!

Copy a Verse or Quote:

_____
_____
_____
_____
_____
_____

Draw Your Plans

To-Do List
_____
_____
_____
_____
_____
_____

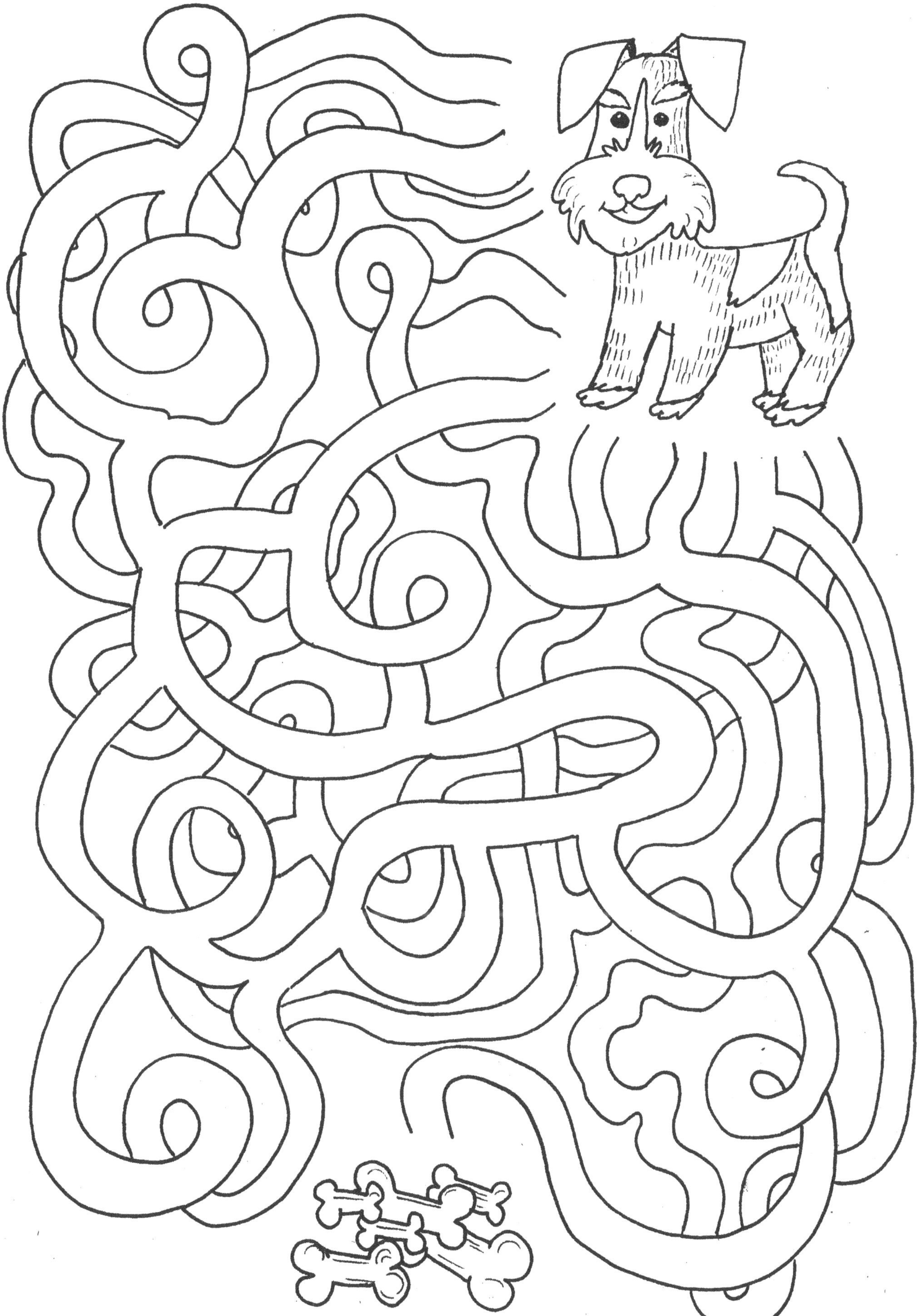

Picture Study

Look closely at this picture.
Think about the lines and shadows.
Practice working with your colored pencils.

Afghan Hound

DRAW THE MISSING PARTS

Use a variety of smooth black drawing pens, with fine points, to complete the picture.

THE DOG SHOP!
YOU HAVE $ 17.50 TO SPEND ON YOUR DOG!

Color the items you will buy
Use a calculator to add up your purchase: $_____
How much change will you receive? $_____

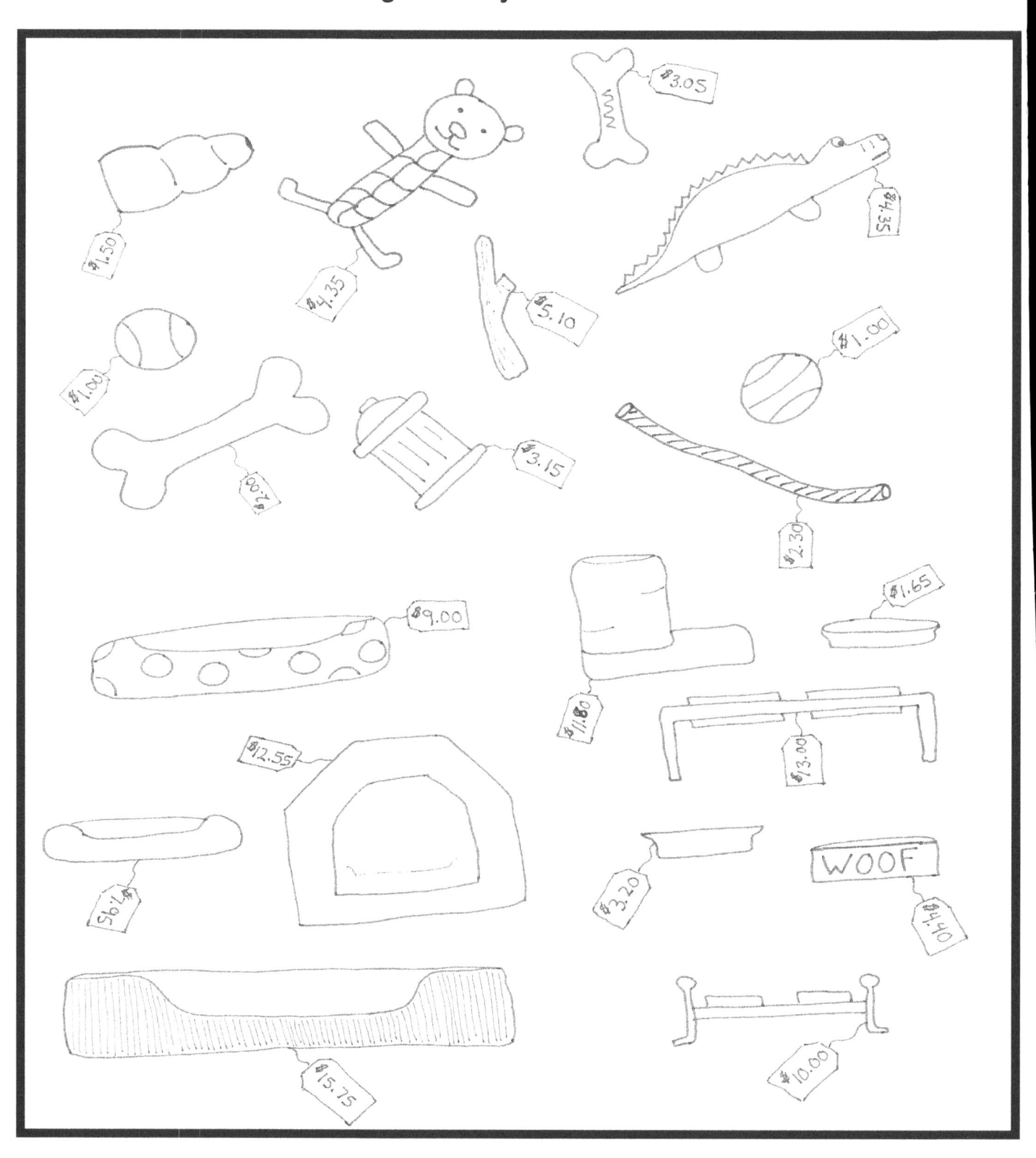

COMPLETE THE COMIC! WHAT HAPPENS NEXT?

READING TIME - 1 HOUR (SET A TIMER)

Choose Four Books - Read from each book for 15 minutes.

Copy important words or pictures from each book here:

Spelling Time

Find 20 Words with 4 letters each.
Look in your books for words.
Write the words here:

_____   _____

_____   _____

_____   _____

_____   _____

_____   _____

_____   _____

_____   _____

_____   _____

_____   _____

_____   _____

Start Time:
_____

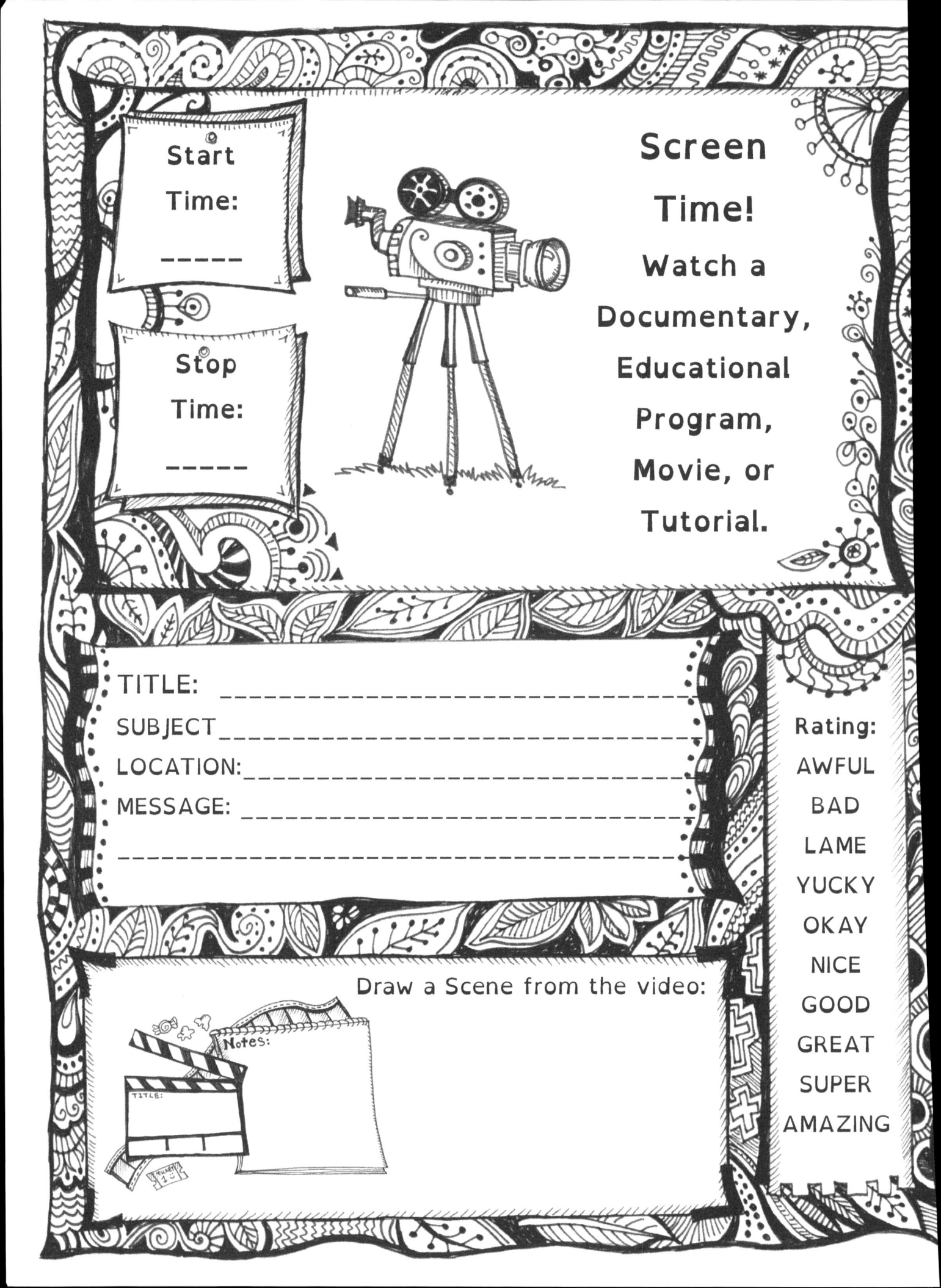

Stop Time:
_____

Screen Time!

Watch a Documentary, Educational Program, Movie, or Tutorial.

TITLE: _____
SUBJECT _____
LOCATION: _____
MESSAGE: _____
_____

Rating:
AWFUL
BAD
LAME
YUCKY
OKAY
NICE
GOOD
GREAT
SUPER
AMAZING

Draw a Scene from the video:

Notes:

TITLE:

Use THIS PAGE for Math Practice
Or be creative and design something, like a dog house!
You could make graphs, maps or geometric designs with this graph paper.

FAMOUS DOGS IN THE HISTORY OF THE WORLD

NAME OF DOG:

TYPE OF DOG:

BEST KNOWN FOR:

DATE OF EVENT:

THE STORY OF THIS INTERESTING DOG:

_____
_____
_____
_____
_____
_____
_____
_____
_____
_____

CIRCLE TODAY'S DATE

January
February
March
April
May
June
July
August
September
October
November
December

1 2 3 4 5 6
7 8 9 10 11
12 13 14 15
16 17 18 19
20 21 22 23
24 25 26 27
28 29 30 31

MONDAY
TUESDAY
WEDNESDAY
THURSDAY
FRIDAY
SATURDAY
SUNDAY

2015
2016
2017
2018
2019
2020
2021
2022
2023
2024
2025
2026
2027
2028
2029

Write Today's Date: _____

START YOUR DAY!

Copy a Verse or Quote:

_____
_____
_____
_____
_____
_____
_____

Draw Your Plans

To-Do List

_____
_____
_____
_____
_____
_____

JUST FOR FUN
ADD 5 DOGS TO THIS PICTURE

Picture Study

Look closely at this picture.

Think about the lines and shadows.

Practice working with your colored pencils.

Japanese Akita

DRAW THE MISSING PARTS

Use a variety of smooth black drawing pens, with fine points, to complete the picture.

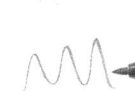

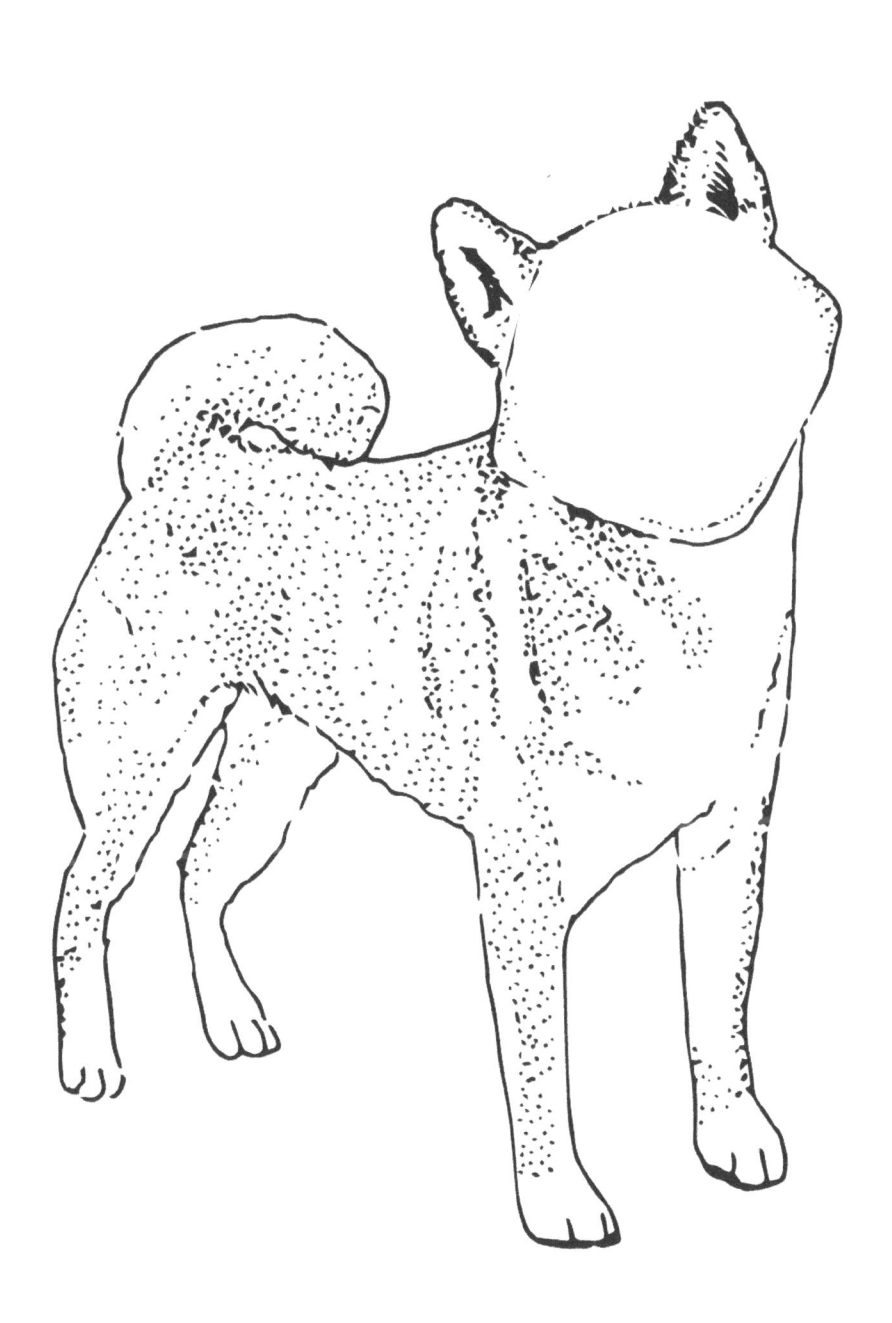

WORKING DOGS

LOOK AT THE PICTURE AND TRY TO ANSWER THESE QUESTIONS:

What type of job is this?

_____

How many dogs and/or people does it take to perform this job?

_____

What types of dogs can do this job?

_____

What special training and commands are required with this job?

_____

Is there special equipment needed for this job?

_____

What is the role of the dogs human partner in this job?

_____

READING TIME - 1 HOUR (SET A TIMER)

Choose Four Books - Read from each book for 15 minutes.

Copy important words or pictures from each book here:

Use THIS PAGE for Math Practice
Or be creative and design something, like a dog house!
You could make graphs, maps or geometric designs with this graph paper.

CIRCLE TODAY'S DATE

January
February
March
April
May
June
July
August
September
October
November
December

1 2 3 4 5 6
7 8 9 10 11
12 13 14 15
16 17 18 19
20 21 22 23
24 25 26 27
28 29 30 31

MONDAY
TUESDAY
WEDNESDAY
THURSDAY
FRIDAY
SATURDAY
SUNDAY

2015
2016
2017
2018
2019
2020
2021
2022
2023
2024
2025
2026
2027
2028
2029

Write Today's Date: _____

START YOUR DAY!

Copy a Verse or Quote:

_____
_____
_____
_____
_____
_____

Draw Your Plans

To-Do List

_____
_____
_____
_____
_____
_____

WORKING DOGS

LOOK AT THE PICTURE AND TRY TO ANSWER THESE QUESTIONS:

What type of job is this?

_____

How many dogs and/or people does it take to perform this job?

_____

What types of dogs can do this job?

_____

What special training and commands are required with this job?

_____

Is there special equipment needed for this job?

_____

What is the role of the dogs human partner in this job?

_____

Picture Study

Look closely at this picture.

Think about the lines and shadows.

Practice working with your colored pencils.

Basset Hound

DRAW THE MISSING PARTS

Use a variety of smooth black drawing pens, with fine points, to complete the picture.

READING TIME - 1 HOUR (SET A TIMER)

Choose Four Books - Read from each book for 15 minutes.

Copy important words or pictures from each book here:

Spelling Time

Find 20 Words with **6** letters each.
Look in your books for words.
Write the words here:

_____   _____

_____   _____

_____   _____

_____   _____

_____   _____

_____   _____

_____   _____

_____   _____

_____   _____

_____   _____

Start Time:
_____

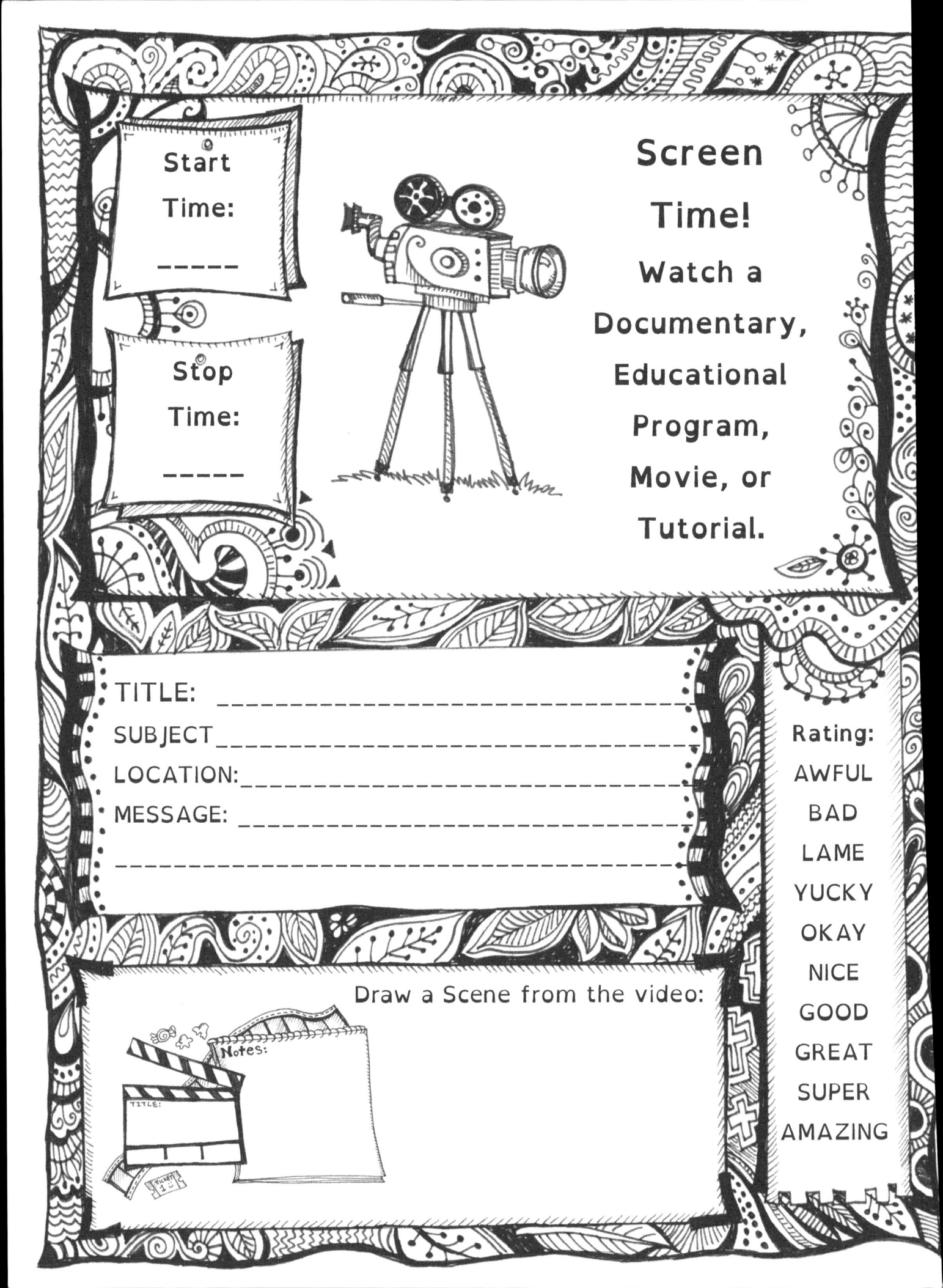

Stop Time:
_____

Screen Time!

Watch a Documentary, Educational Program, Movie, or Tutorial.

TITLE: _____
SUBJECT _____
LOCATION: _____
MESSAGE: _____
_____

Rating:
AWFUL
BAD
LAME
YUCKY
OKAY
NICE
GOOD
GREAT
SUPER
AMAZING

Draw a Scene from the video:

Notes:

TITLE:

CHOOSE A DOG BREED:

Where does this breed originally come from?
_____
_____

What are some special traits specific to this breed?
_____
_____

Are there any famous dogs that were this breed?
_____
_____

What else did you find out?
_____
_____

DRAW THE BREED:

DRAW ANYTHING!

CIRCLE TODAY'S DATE

January
February
March
April
May
June
July
August
September
October
November
December

1 2 3 4 5 6
7 8 9 10 11
12 13 14 15
16 17 18 19
20 21 22 23
24 25 26 27
28 29 30 31

MONDAY
TUESDAY
WEDNESDAY
THURSDAY
FRIDAY
SATURDAY
SUNDAY

2015
2016
2017
2018
2019
2020
2021
2022
2023
2024
2025
2026
2027
2028
2029

Write Today's Date: _____

START YOUR DAY!

Copy a Verse or Quote:

_____
_____
_____
_____
_____
_____
_____

Draw Your Plans

To-Do List

_____
_____
_____
_____
_____
_____

COMPLETE THE COMIC! WHAT HAPPENS NEXT?

Picture Study

Look closely at this picture.

Think about the lines and shadows.

Practice working with your colored pencils.

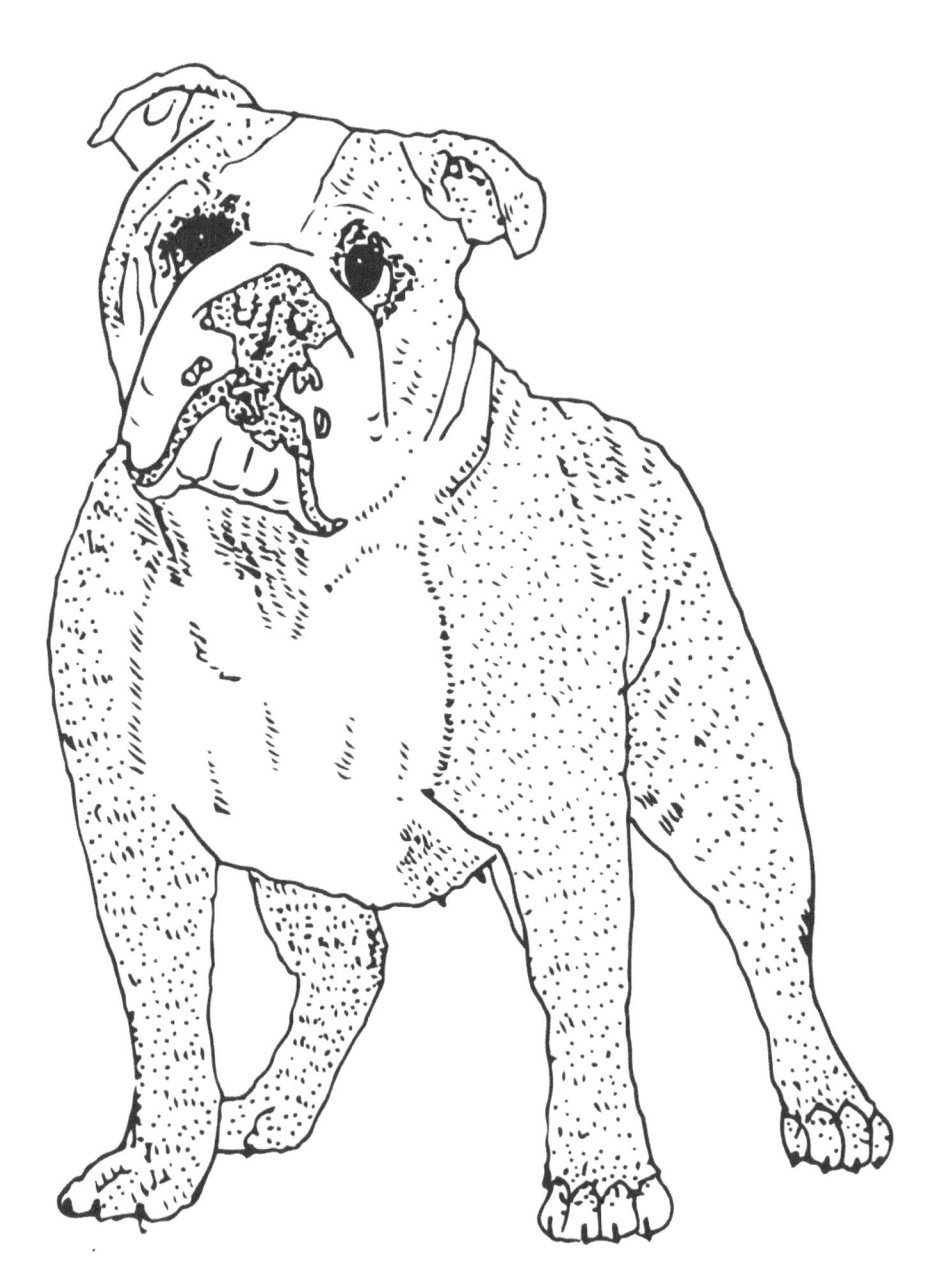

Bulldog

DRAW THE MISSING PARTS

Use a variety of smooth black drawing pens, with fine points, to complete the picture.

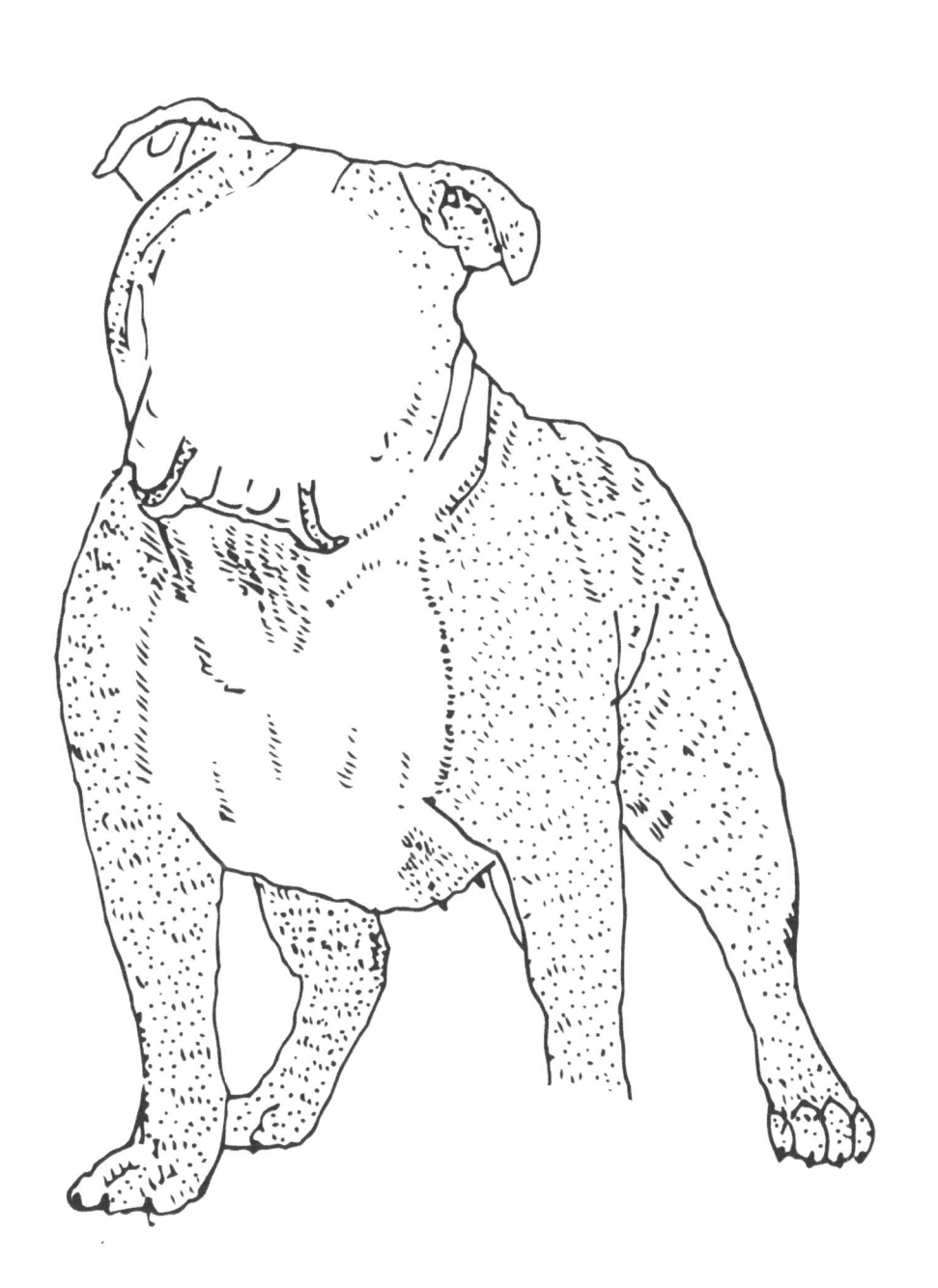

WORKING DOGS

LOOK AT THE PICTURE AND TRY TO ANSWER THESE QUESTIONS:

What type of job is this?

_____

How many dogs and/or people does it take to perform this job?

_____

What types of dogs can do this job?

_____

What special training and commands are required with this job?

_____

Is there special equipment needed for this job?

_____

What is the role of the dogs human partner in this job?

_____

READING TIME - 1 HOUR (SET A TIMER)

Choose Four Books - Read from each book for 15 minutes.

Copy important words or pictures from each book here:

COLOR WITH A FRIEND

SHARE THIS PAGE

Use THIS PAGE for Math Practice
Or be creative and design something, like a dog house!
You could make graphs, maps or geometric designs with this graph paper.

CHOOSE A DOG BREED:

Where does this breed originally come from?
_____
_____

What are some special traits specific to this breed?
_____
_____

Are there any famous dogs that were this breed?
_____
_____

What else did you find out?
_____
_____

DRAW THE BREED:

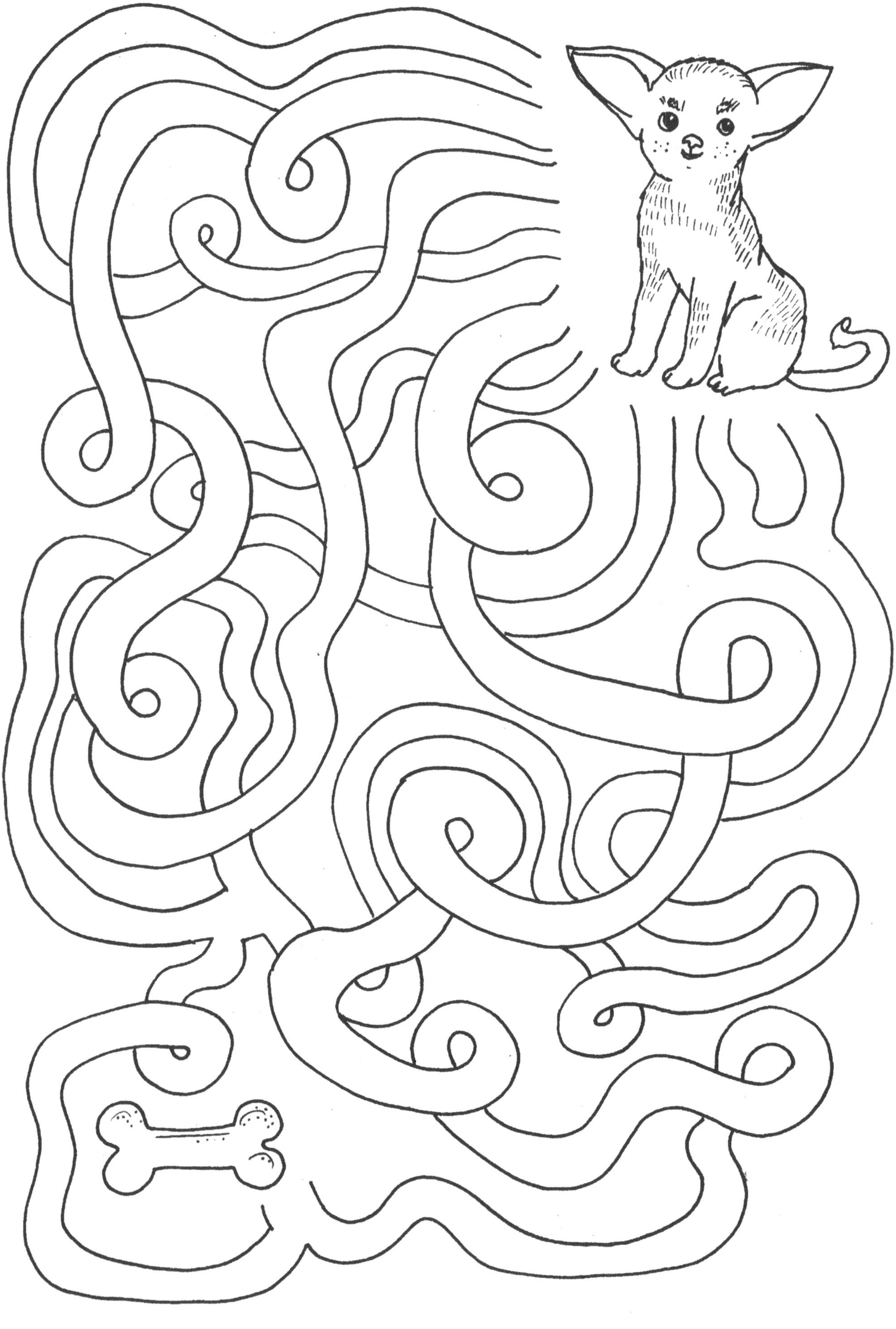

CIRCLE TODAY'S DATE

January
February
March
April
May
June
July
August
September
October
November
December

1 2 3 4 5 6
7 8 9 10 11
12 13 14 15
16 17 18 19
20 21 22 23
24 25 26 27
28 29 30 31

MONDAY
TUESDAY
WEDNESDAY
THURSDAY
FRIDAY
SATURDAY
SUNDAY

2015
2016
2017
2018
2019
2020
2021
2022
2023
2024
2025
2026
2027
2028
2029

Write Today's Date: _____

Picture Study

Look closely at this picture.
Think about the lines and shadows.
Practice working with your colored pencils.

Bull Terrier

DRAW THE MISSING PARTS

Use a variety of smooth black drawing pens, with fine points, to complete the picture.

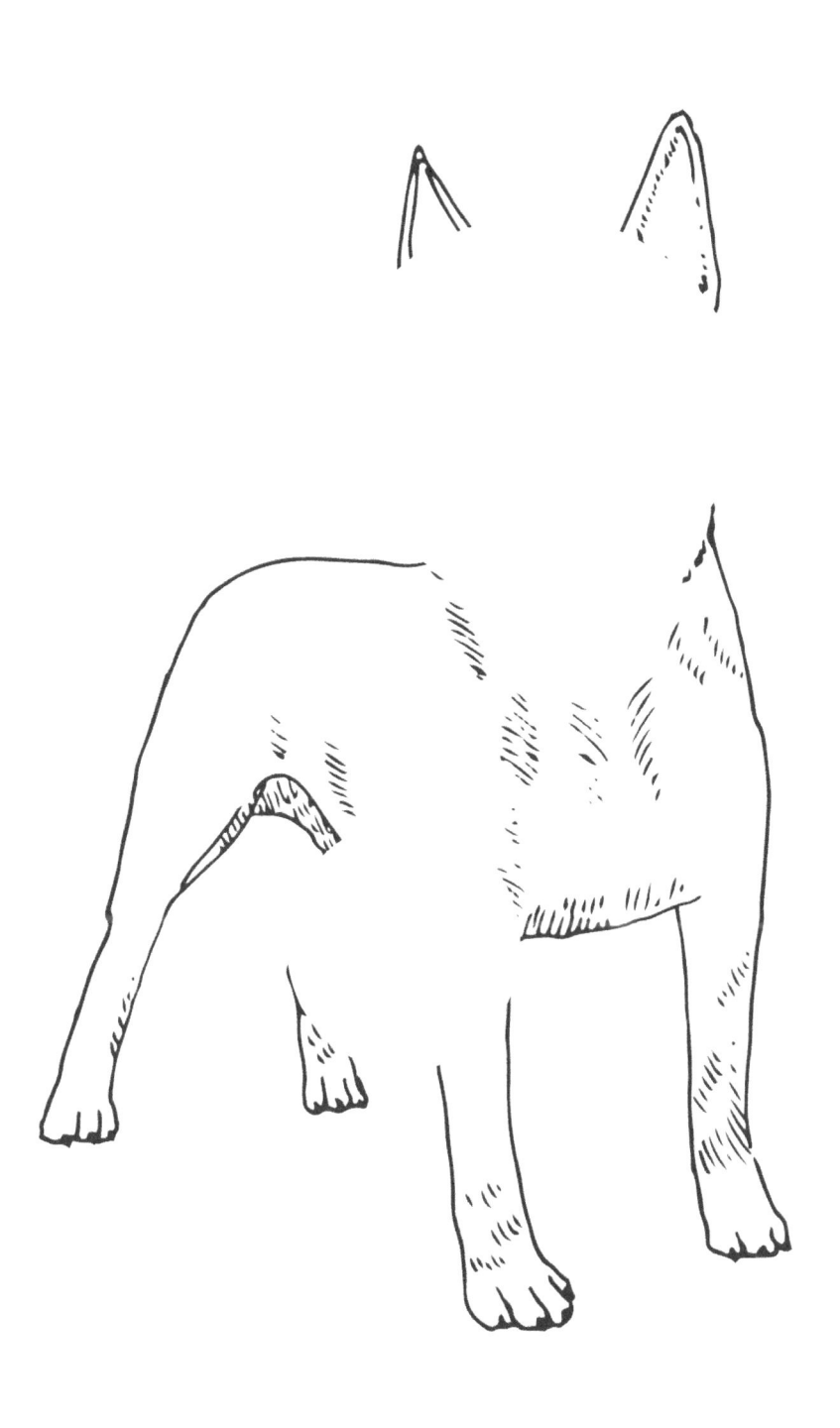

WORKING DOGS

LOOK AT THE PICTURE AND TRY TO ANSWER THESE QUESTIONS:

What type of job is this?

_____

How many dogs and/or people does it take to perform this job?

_____

What types of dogs can do this job?

_____

What special training and commands are required with this job?

_____

Is there special equipment needed for this job?

_____

What is the role of the dogs human partner in this job?

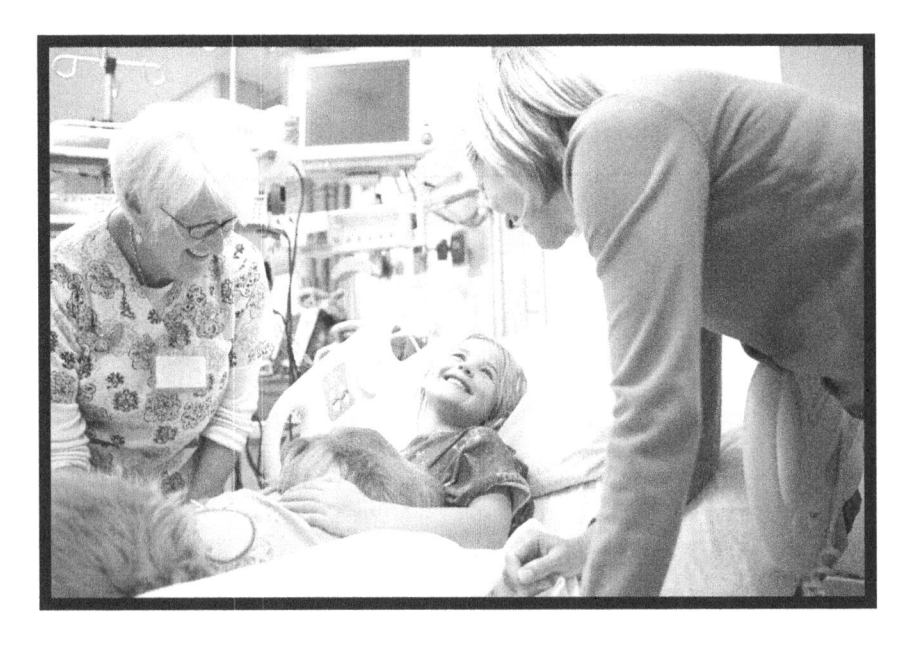

_____

READING TIME - 1 HOUR (SET A TIMER)

Choose Four Books - Read from each book for 15 minutes.

Copy important words or pictures from each book here:

Spelling Time

Find 20 Words with 8 letters each.
Look in your books for words.
Write the words here:

_____   _____

_____   _____

_____   _____

_____   _____

_____   _____

_____   _____

_____   _____

_____   _____

_____   _____

_____   _____

Start Time:

Stop Time:

Screen Time!

Watch a Documentary, Educational Program, Movie, or Tutorial.

TITLE: _____
SUBJECT _____
LOCATION: _____
MESSAGE: _____
_____

Rating:
AWFUL
BAD
LAME
YUCKY
OKAY
NICE
GOOD
GREAT
SUPER
AMAZING

Draw a Scene from the video:

Notes:

TITLE:

WORKING WITH DOGS

CAREERS WITH DOGS

LOOK AT THE PICTURE AND TRY TO ANSWER THESE QUESTIONS:

What type of job is this?

_____

What kind of training does a person need to do this job?

_____

What kinds of dogs are involved in this job?

_____

Is there special equipment needed for this job?

_____

How much money does a person earn for doing this job?

_____

Is this a job you would like to do? Why or why not?

_____
_____
_____
_____
_____
_____
_____
_____
_____

CIRCLE TODAY'S DATE

January
February
March
April
May
June
July
August
September
October
November
December

1 2 3 4 5 6
7 8 9 10 11
12 13 14 15
16 17 18 19
20 21 22 23
24 25 26 27
28 29 30 31

MONDAY
TUESDAY
WEDNESDAY
THURSDAY
FRIDAY
SATURDAY
SUNDAY

2015
2016
2017
2018
2019
2020
2021
2022
2023
2024
2025
2026
2027
2028
2029

Write Today's Date: _ _ _ _ _ _ _ _ _ _ _ _ _ _

START YOUR DAY!

Copy a Verse or Quote:

_____
_____
_____
_____
_____
_____
_____

Draw Your Plans

To-Do List

_____
_____
_____
_____
_____

Picture Study

Look closely at this picture.
Think about the lines and shadows.
Practice working with your colored pencils.

Cocker Spaniel

DRAW THE MISSING PARTS

Use a variety of smooth black drawing pens, with fine points, to complete the picture.

WORKING DOGS

LOOK AT THE PICTURE AND TRY TO ANSWER THESE QUESTIONS:

What type of job is this?

_____

How many dogs and/or people does it take to perform this job?

_____

What types of dogs can do this job?

_____

What special training and commands are required with this job?

_____

Is there special equipment needed for this job?

_____

What is the role of the dogs human partner in this job?

_____

DRAW ME!

READING TIME - 1 HOUR (SET A TIMER)

Choose Four Books - Read from each book for 15 minutes.

Copy important words or pictures from each book here:

Spelling Time

Find 20 Words with 9 letters each.
Look in your books for words.
Write the words here:

_____   _____
_____   _____
_____   _____
_____   _____
_____   _____
_____   _____
_____   _____
_____   _____
_____   _____
_____   _____

World News Today!

Talk to your parents about current events.

Look at a newspaper, news broadcast or website.

Color the countries you learn about.

Tell the news stories with words or pictures.

WORKING WITH DOGS

CAREERS WITH DOGS

LOOK AT THE PICTURE AND TRY TO ANSWER THESE QUESTIONS:

What type of job is this?

_____

What kind of training does a person need to do this job?

_____

What kinds of dogs are involved in this job?

_____

Is there special equipment needed for this job?

_____

How much money does a person earn for doing this job?

_____

Is this a job you would like to do? Why or why not?

_____
_____
_____
_____
_____
_____
_____
_____
_____

CIRCLE TODAY'S DATE

January
February
March
April
May
June
July
August
September
October
November
December

1 2 3 4 5 6
7 8 9 10 11
12 13 14 15
16 17 18 19
20 21 22 23
24 25 26 27
28 29 30 31

MONDAY
TUESDAY
WEDNESDAY
THURSDAY
FRIDAY
SATURDAY
SUNDAY

2015
2016
2017
2018
2019
2020
2021
2022
2023
2024
2025
2026
2027
2028
2029

Write Today's Date: _____

START YOUR DAY!

Copy a Verse or Quote:

_____
_____
_____
_____
_____
_____
_____

Draw Your Plans

To-Do List

_____
_____
_____
_____
_____
_____

Picture Study

Look closely at this picture.

Think about the lines and shadows.

Practice working with your colored pencils.

Dalmatian

DRAW THE MISSING PARTS

Use a variety of smooth black drawing pens, with fine points, to complete the picture.

THE DOG SHOP!
YOU HAVE $30.50 TO SPEND ON YOUR DOG!

Color the items you will buy
Use a calculator to add up your purchase: $_____
How much change will you receive? $_____

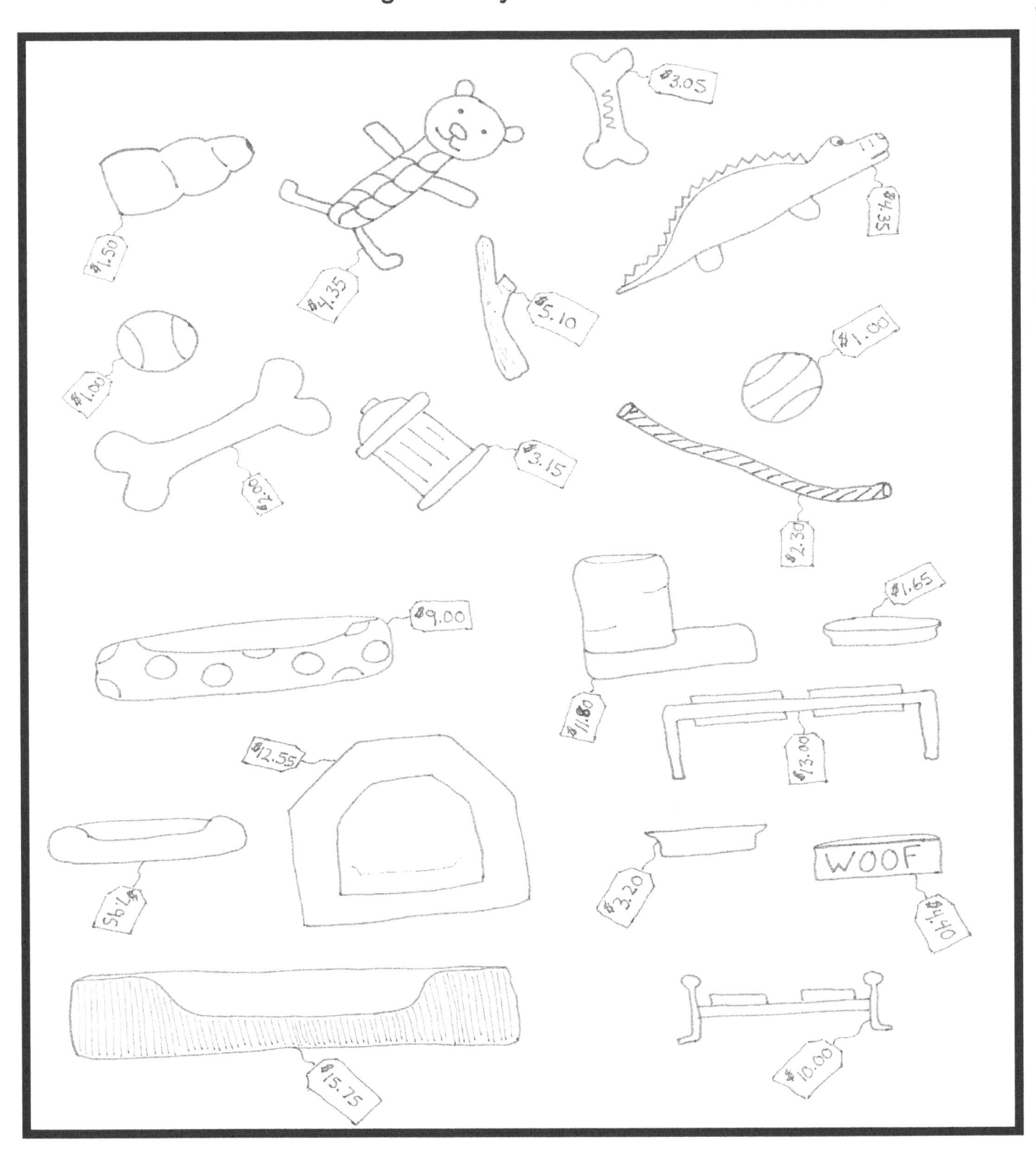

COMPLETE THE COMIC! WHAT HAPPENS NEXT?

WORKING DOGS

LOOK AT THE PICTURE AND TRY TO ANSWER THESE QUESTIONS:

What type of job is this?

_____

How many dogs and/or people does it take to perform this job?

_____

What types of dogs can do this job?

_____

What special training and commands are required with this job?

_____

Is there special equipment needed for this job?

_____

What is the role of the dogs human partner in this job?

_____

DRAW ME!

READING TIME - 1 HOUR (SET A TIMER)

Choose Four Books - Read from each book for 15 minutes.

Copy important words or pictures from each book here:

WORKING WITH DOGS

CAREERS WITH DOGS

LOOK AT THE PICTURE AND TRY TO ANSWER THESE QUESTIONS:

What type of job is this?

_____

What kind of training does a person need to do this job?

_____

What kinds of dogs are involved in this job?

_____

Is there special equipment needed for this job?

_____

How much money does a person earn for doing this job?

_____

Is this a job you would like to do? Why or why not?

_____
_____
_____
_____
_____
_____
_____
_____
_____

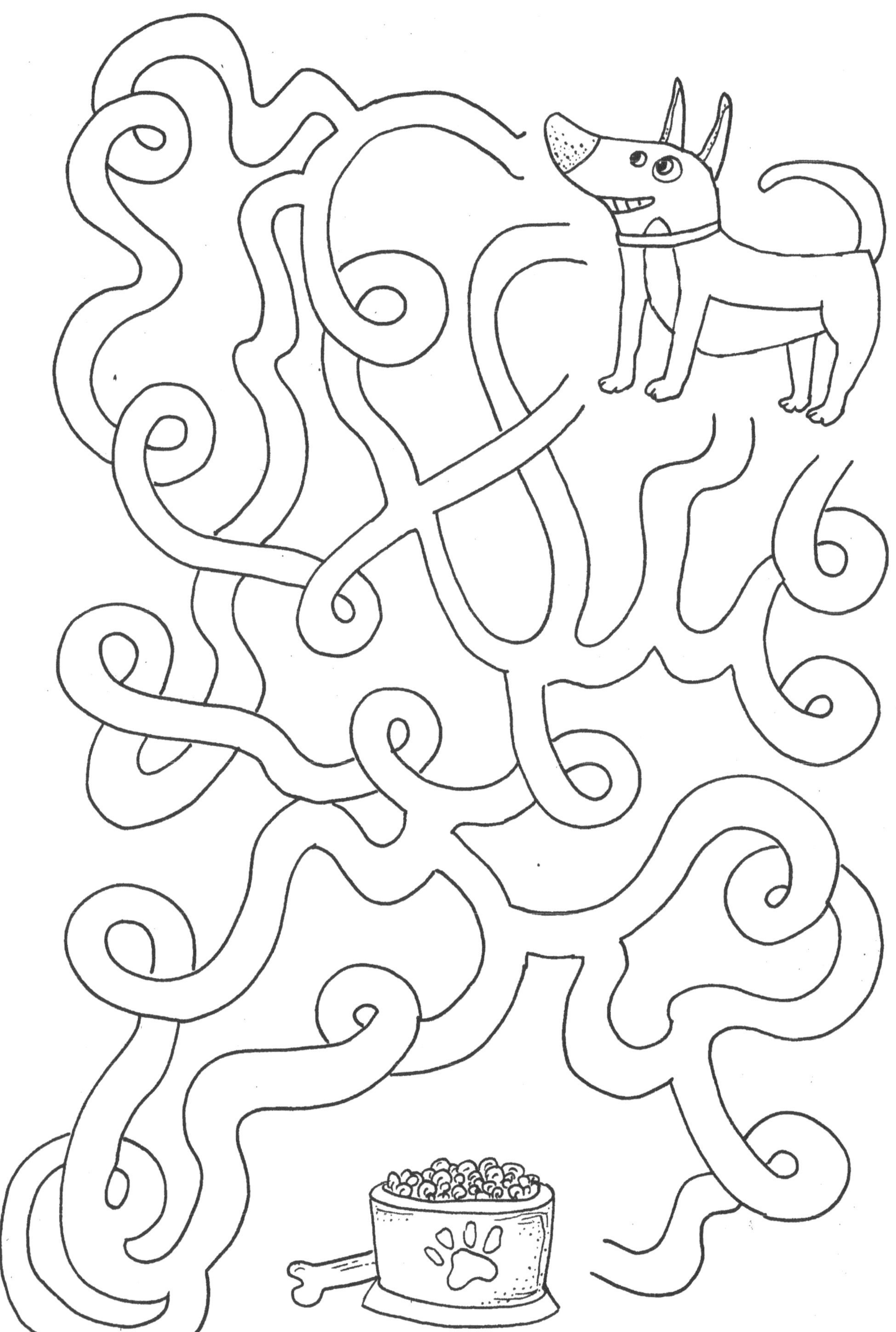

DOGS IN HISTORY!
ADD CLIP ART, DRAWINGS, PICTURES OR PHOTOS

CIRCLE TODAY'S DATE

January
February
March
April
May
June
July
August
September
October
November
December

1 2 3 4 5 6
7 8 9 10 11
12 13 14 15
16 17 18 19
20 21 22 23
24 25 26 27
28 29 30 31

MONDAY
TUESDAY
WEDNESDAY
THURSDAY
FRIDAY
SATURDAY
SUNDAY

2015
2016
2017
2018
2019
2020
2021
2022
2023
2024
2025
2026
2027
2028
2029

Write Today's Date: _ _ _ _ _ _ _ _ _ _ _ _ _ _

START YOUR DAY!

Copy a Verse or Quote:

_____
_____
_____
_____
_____
_____

Draw Your Plans

To-Do List

_____
_____
_____
_____
_____
_____

Picture Study

Look closely at this picture.

Think about the lines and shadows.

Practice working with your colored pencils.

Dachshund

DRAW THE MISSING PARTS

Use a variety of smooth black drawing pens, with fine points, to complete the picture.

JUST FOR FUN! COLOR MY COAT

READING TIME - 1 HOUR (SET A TIMER)

Choose Four Books - Read from each book for 15 minutes.

Copy important words or pictures from each book here:

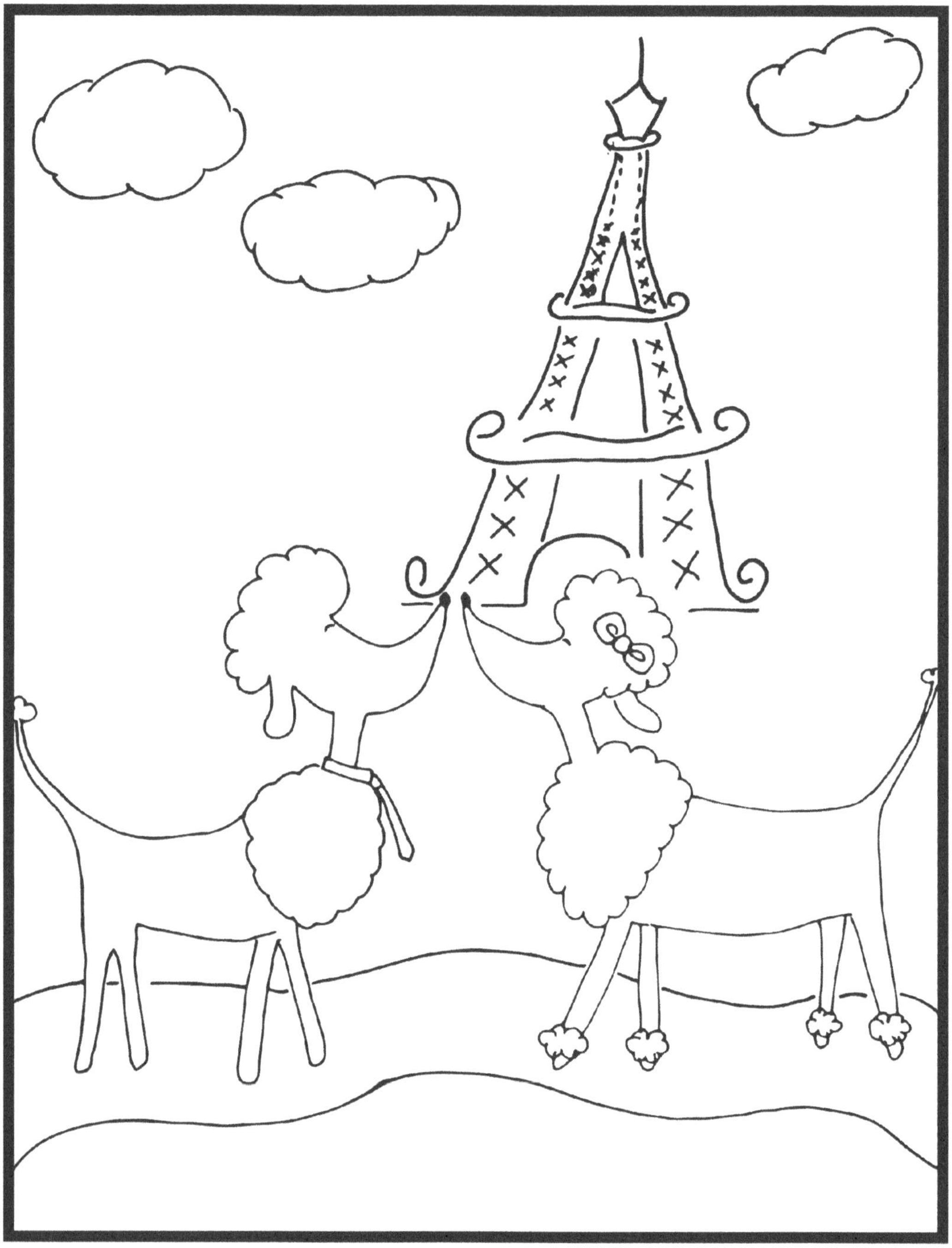

Start Time: _____

Stop Time: _____

Screen Time!

Watch a Documentary, Educational Program, Movie, or Tutorial.

TITLE: _____
SUBJECT _____
LOCATION: _____
MESSAGE: _____
_____

Rating:
AWFUL
BAD
LAME
YUCKY
OKAY
NICE
GOOD
GREAT
SUPER
AMAZING

Draw a Scene from the video:

Notes:
TITLE:

Use THIS PAGE for Math Practice
Or be creative and design something, like a dog house!
You could make graphs, maps or geometric designs with this graph paper.

Listening Time

Listen to an audio book or classical music or ask someone to read a story to you while you color and draw on the next page.

What are you listening to?

_____

CHOOSE A DOG BREED:

Where does this breed originally come from?

What are some special traits specific to this breed?

Are there any famous dogs that were this breed?

What else did you find out?

DRAW THE BREED:

JUST FOR FUN
ADD 10 DOGS TO THIS PICTURE

COLOR WITH A FRIEND

SHARE THIS PAGE

CIRCLE TODAY'S DATE

January
February
March
April
May
June
July
August
September
October
November
December

1 2 3 4 5 6
7 8 9 10 11
12 13 14 15
16 17 18 19
20 21 22 23
24 25 26 27
28 29 30 31

MONDAY
TUESDAY
WEDNESDAY
THURSDAY
FRIDAY
SATURDAY
SUNDAY

2015
2016
2017
2018
2019
2020
2021
2022
2023
2024
2025
2026
2027
2028
2029

Write Today's Date: _ _ _ _ _ _ _ _ _ _ _ _ _

START YOUR DAY!

Copy a Verse or Quote:

_____
_____
_____
_____
_____
_____

Draw Your Plans

To-Do List

_____
_____
_____
_____
_____
_____

Picture Study

Look closely at this picture.
Think about the lines and shadows.
Practice working with your colored pencils.

German Shepherd

DRAW THE MISSING PARTS

Use a variety of smooth black drawing pens, with fine points, to complete the picture.

WORKING DOGS

LOOK AT THE PICTURE AND TRY TO ANSWER THESE QUESTIONS:

What type of job is this?

_____

How many dogs and/or people does it take to perform this job?

_____

What types of dogs can do this job?

_____

What special training and commands are required with this job?

_____

Is there special equipment needed for this job?

_____

What is the role of the dogs human partner in this job?

_____

READING TIME - 1 HOUR (SET A TIMER)

Choose Four Books - Read from each book for 15 minutes.

Copy important words or pictures from each book here:

Spelling Time

Find 20 Words with **6** letters each.
Look in your books for words.
Write the words here:

_____   _____

_____   _____

_____   _____

_____   _____

_____   _____

_____   _____

_____   _____

_____   _____

_____   _____

_____   _____

Start Time:
_____

Stop Time:
_____

Screen Time!

Watch a Documentary, Educational Program, Movie, or Tutorial.

TITLE: _____
SUBJECT _____
LOCATION: _____
MESSAGE: _____
_____

Rating:
AWFUL
BAD
LAME
YUCKY
OKAY
NICE
GOOD
GREAT
SUPER
AMAZING

Draw a Scene from the video:

Notes:

TITLE:

Use THIS PAGE for Math Practice
Or be creative and design something, like a dog house!
You could make graphs, maps or geometric designs with this graph paper.

START YOUR DAY!

Copy a Verse or Quote:

_____
_____
_____
_____
_____
_____

Draw Your Plans

To-Do List

_____
_____
_____
_____
_____
_____

Picture Study

Look closely at this picture.

Think about the lines and shadows.

Practice working with your colored pencils.

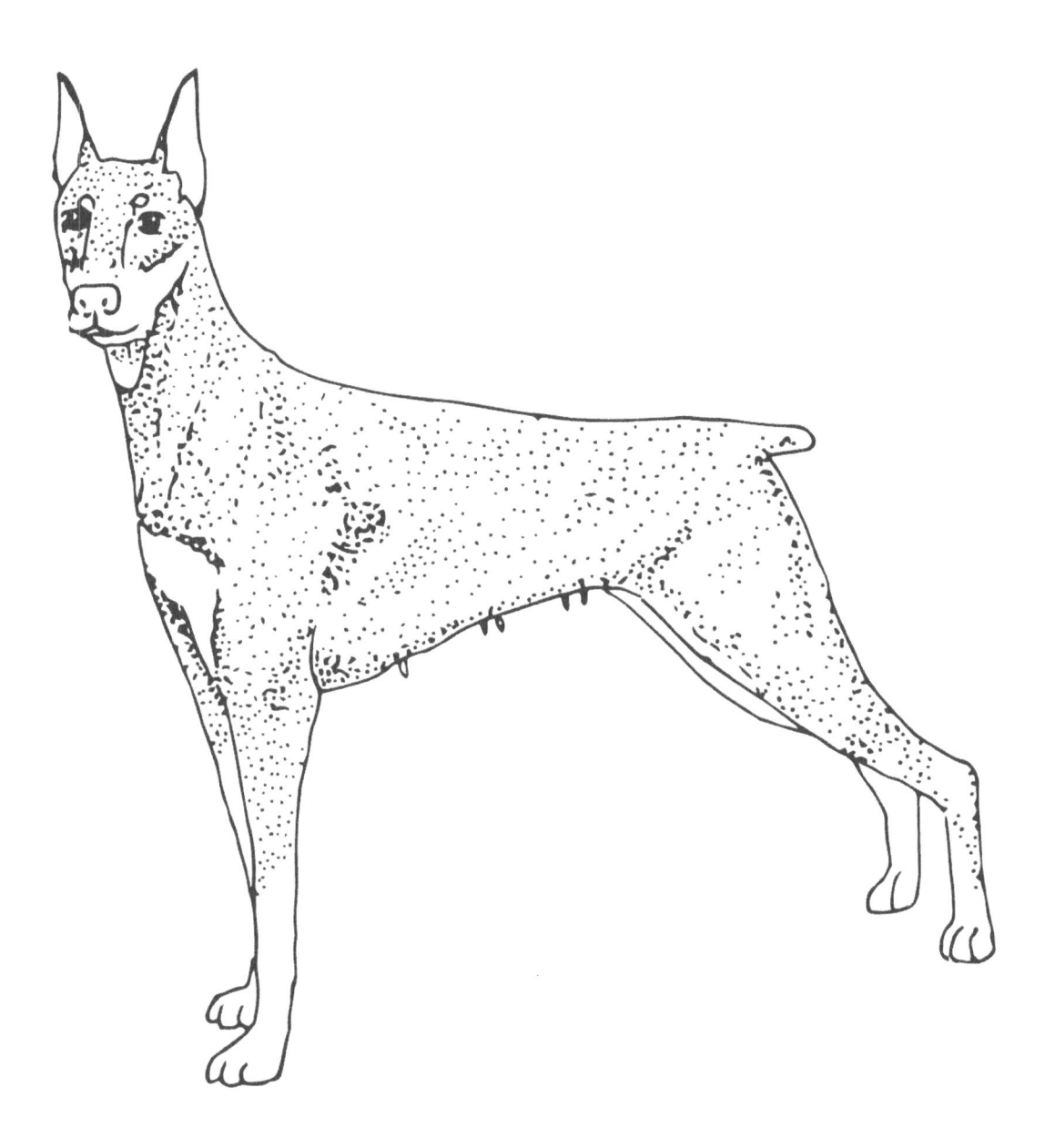

Doberman

DRAW THE MISSING PARTS

Use a variety of smooth black drawing pens, with fine points, to complete the picture.

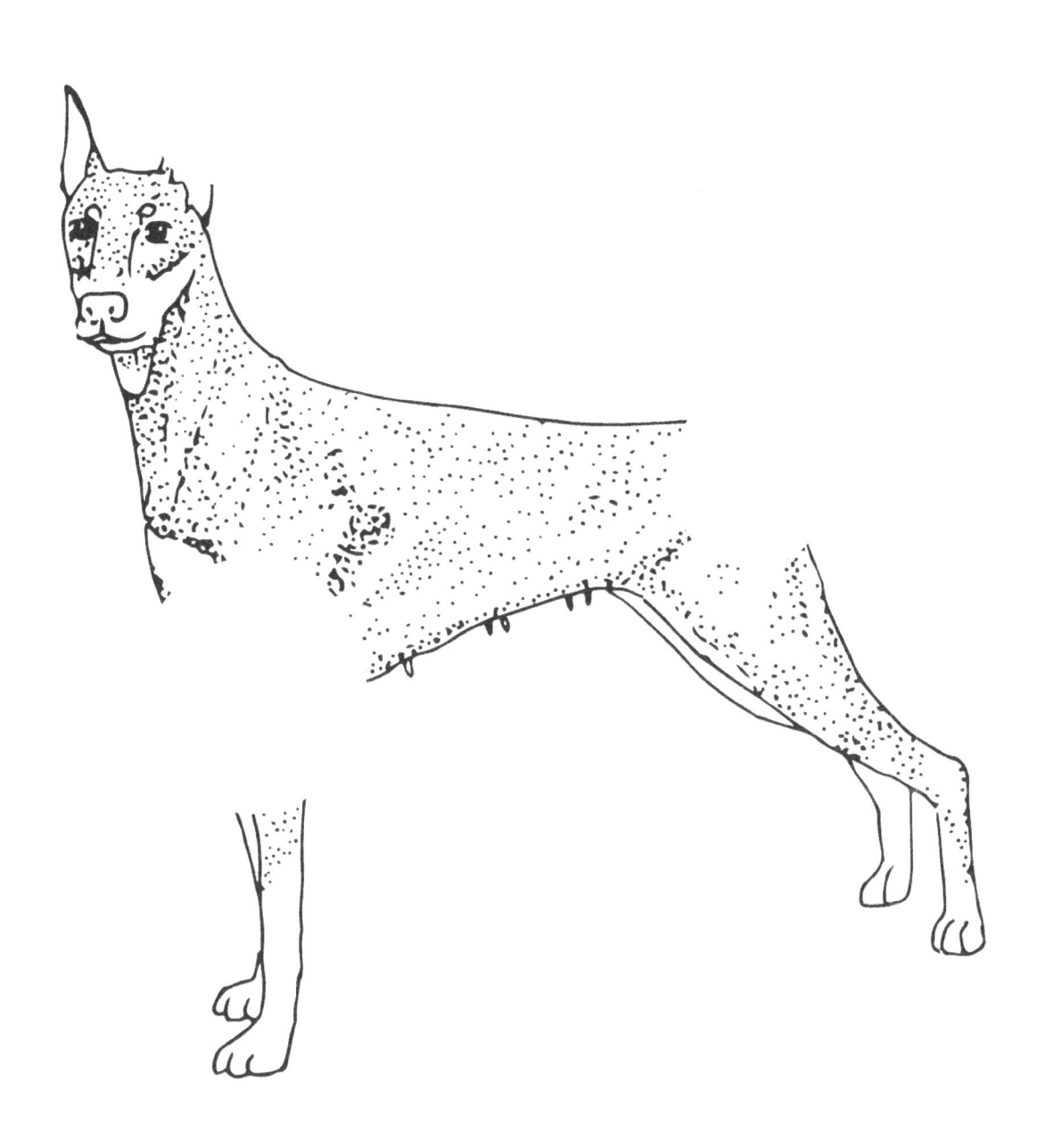

Retrieve

open

Comfort

alert

READING TIME - 1 HOUR (SET A TIMER)

Choose Four Books - Read from each book for 15 minutes.

Copy important words or pictures from each book here:

Spelling Time

Find 20 Words with 5 letters each.
Look in your books for words.
Write the words here:

_____   _____

_____   _____

_____   _____

_____   _____

_____   _____

_____   _____

_____   _____

_____   _____

_____   _____

_____   _____

World News Today!

Talk to your parents about current events.

Look at a newspaper, news broadcast or website.

Color the countries you learn about.

Tell the news stories with words or pictures.

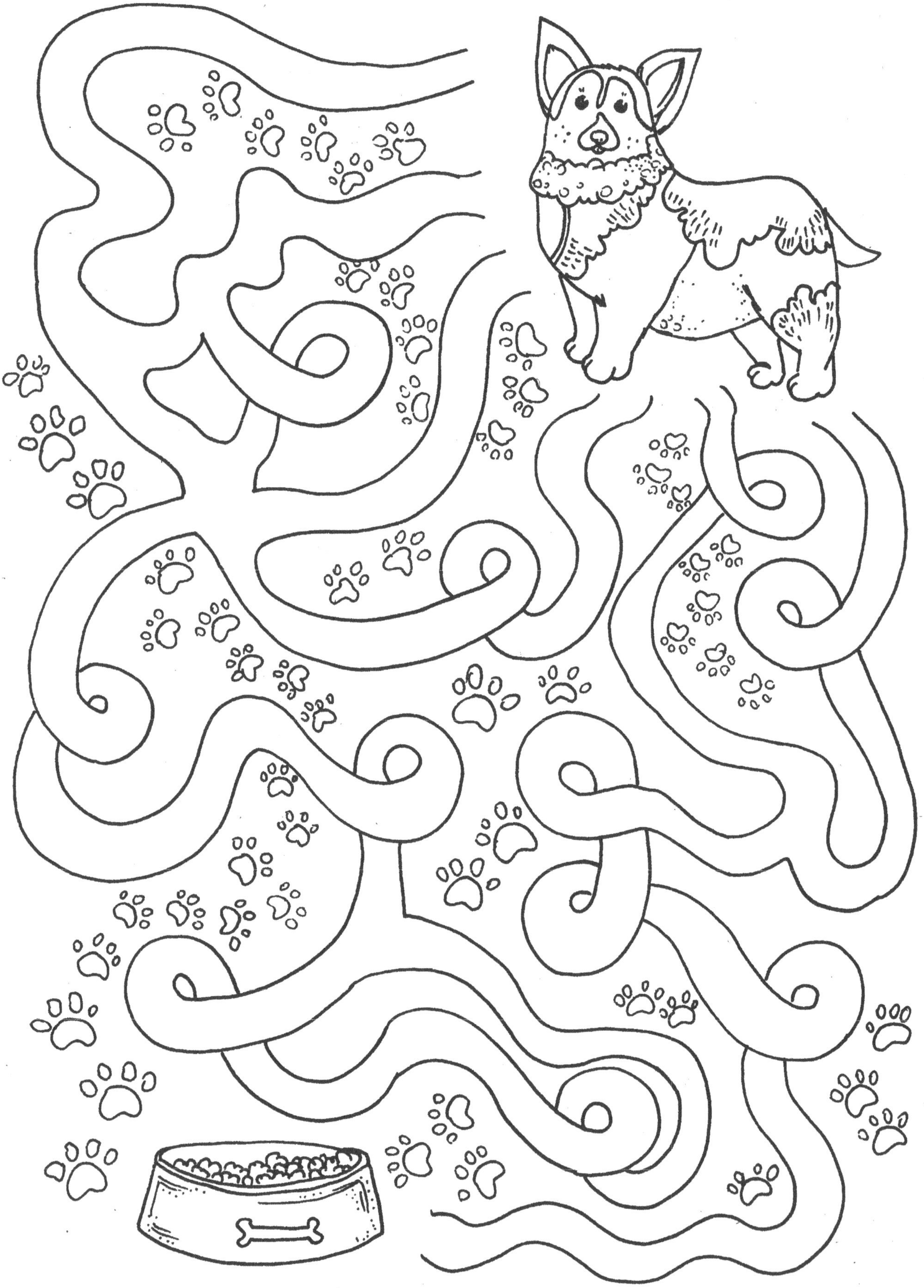

CIRCLE TODAY'S DATE

January
February
March
April
May
June
July
August
September
October
November
December

1 2 3 4 5 6
7 8 9 10 11
12 13 14 15
16 17 18 19
20 21 22 23
24 25 26 27
28 29 30 31

MONDAY
TUESDAY
WEDNESDAY
THURSDAY
FRIDAY
SATURDAY
SUNDAY

2015
2016
2017
2018
2019
2020
2021
2022
2023
2024
2025
2026
2027
2028
2029

Write Today's Date: _ _ _ _ _ _ _ _ _ _ _ _ _ _

START YOUR DAY!

Copy a Verse or Quote:

_____
_____
_____
_____
_____
_____
_____

Draw Your Plans

To-Do List

_____
_____
_____
_____
_____

WORKING DOGS

LOOK AT THE PICTURE AND TRY TO ANSWER THESE QUESTIONS:

What type of job is this?

_____

How many dogs and/or people does it take to perform this job?

_____

What types of dogs can do this job?

_____

What special training and commands are required with this job?

_____

Is there special equipment needed for this job?

_____

What is the role of the dogs human partner in this job?

_____

READING TIME – 1 HOUR (SET A TIMER)

Choose Four Books - Read from each book for 15 minutes.

Copy important words or pictures from each book here:

DOGS IN HISTORY!
ADD CLIP ART, DRAWINGS, PICTURES OR PHOTOS

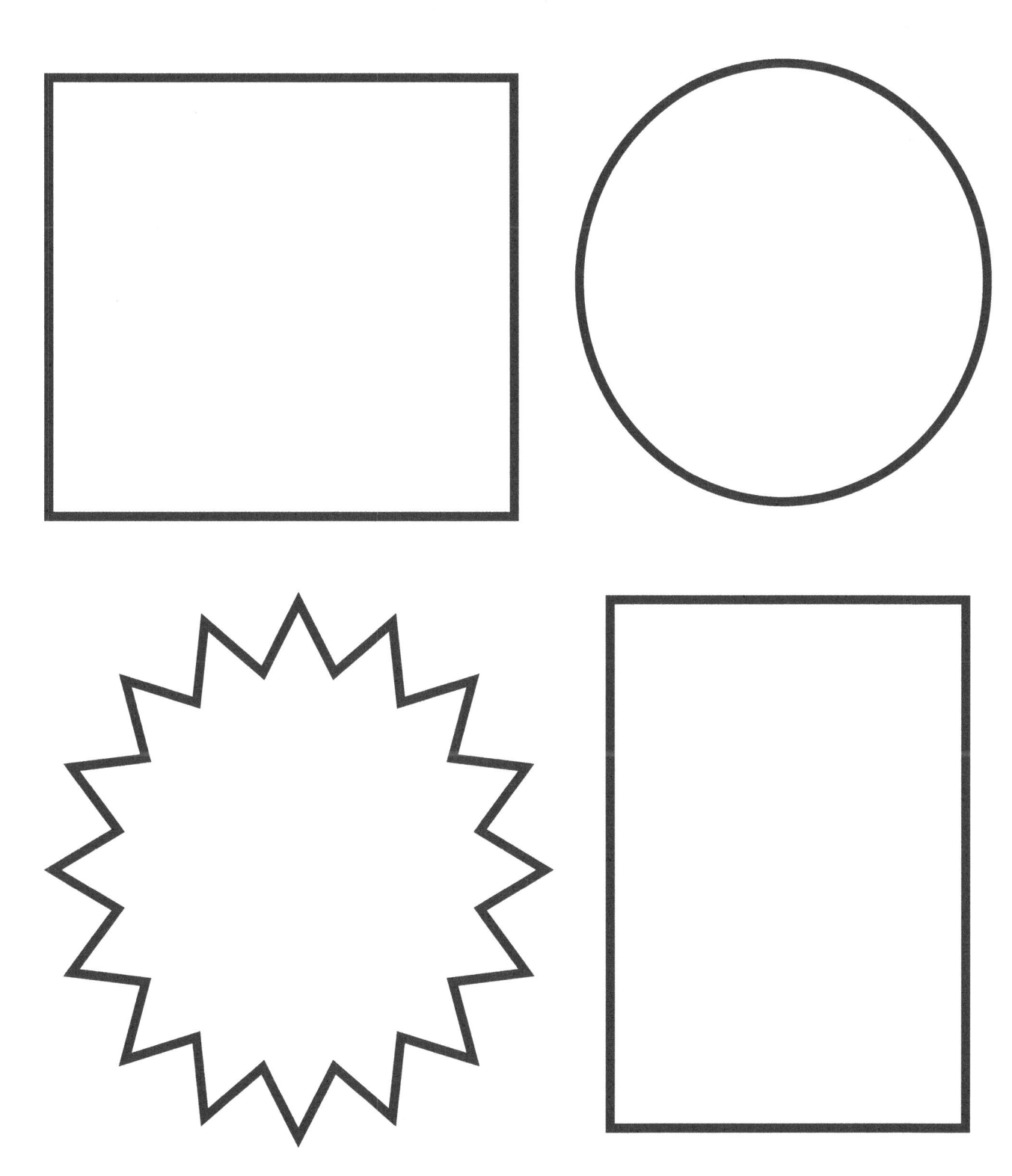

THE DOG SHOP!
YOU HAVE $70.50 TO SPEND ON YOUR DOG!

Color the items you will buy
Use a calculator to add up your purchase: $_____
How much change will you receive? $_____

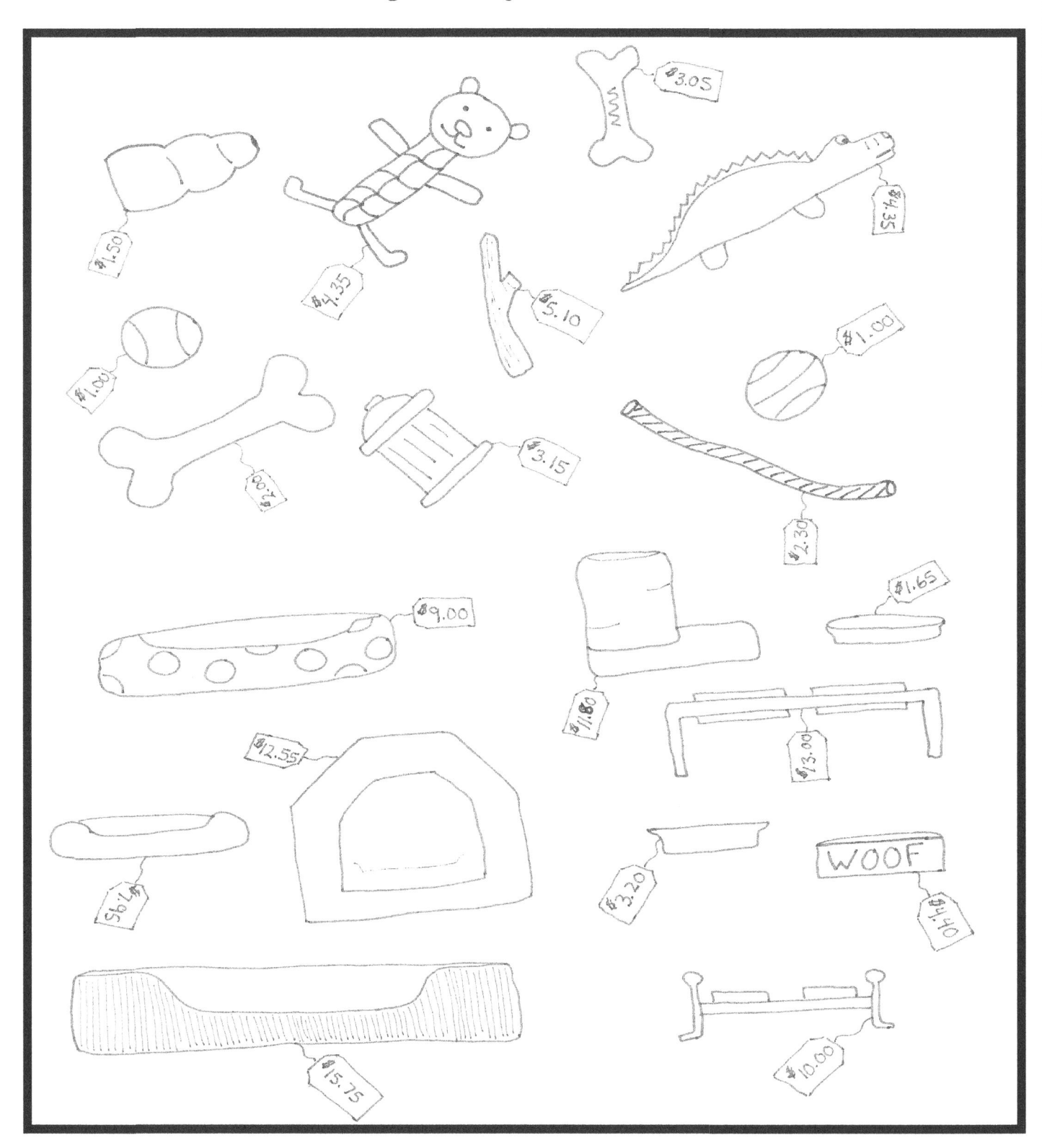

- $3.05
- $1.50
- $4.35
- $4.35
- $5.10
- $1.00
- $1.00
- $2.00
- $3.15
- $2.30
- $1.65
- $9.00
- $11.80
- $13.00
- $12.55
- $7.95
- $3.20
- $4.40
- $15.75
- $10.00

COMPLETE THE COMIC! WHAT HAPPENS NEXT?

Fun Writing Practice:

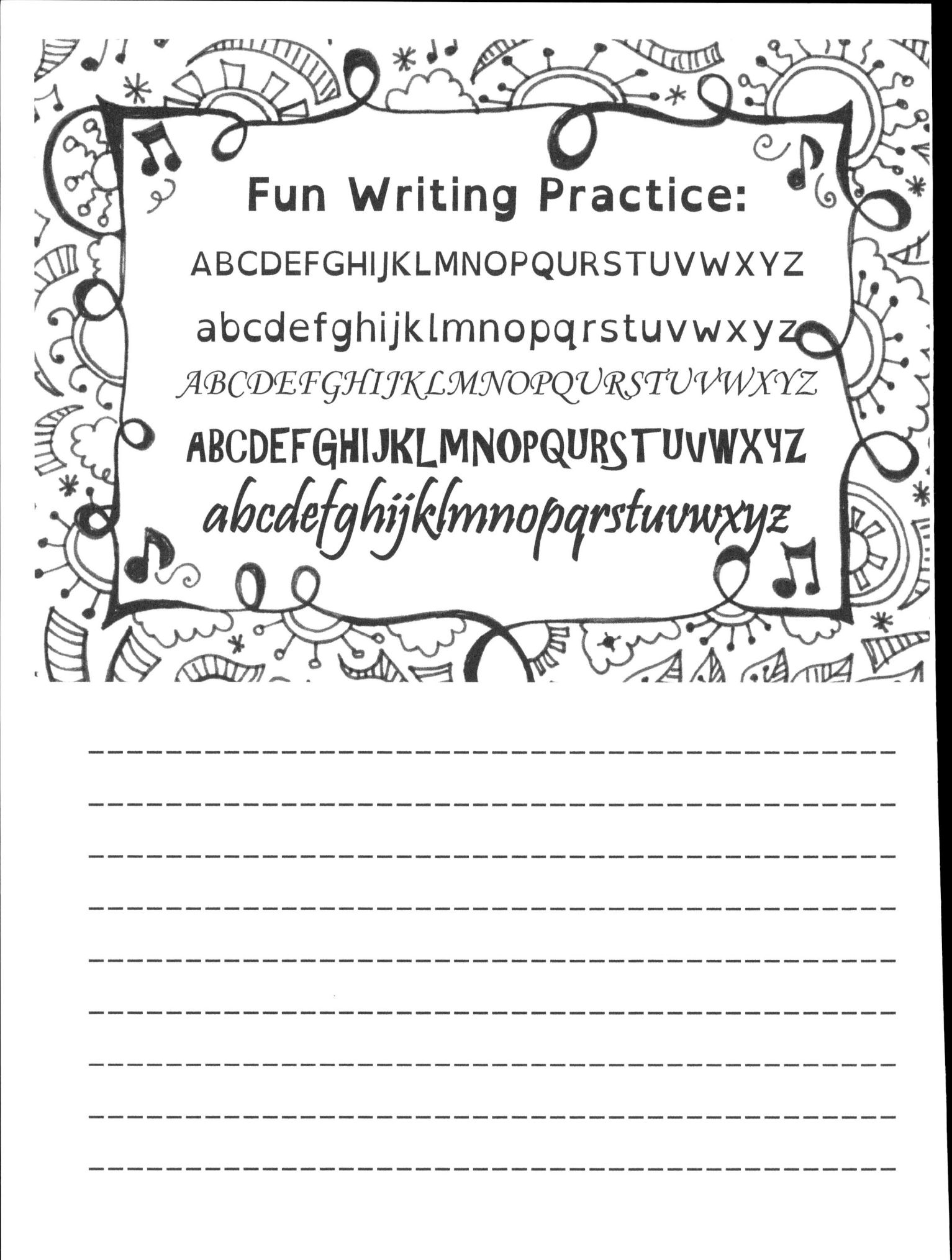

ABCDEFGHIJKLMNOPQURSTUVWXYZ

abcdefghijklmnopqrstuvwxyz

ABCDEFGHIJKLMNOPQURSTUVWXYZ

ABCDEFGHIJKLMNOPQURSTUVWXYZ

abcdefghijklmnopqrstuvwxyz

CIRCLE TODAY'S DATE

January
February
March
April
May
June
July
August
September
October
November
December

1 2 3 4 5 6
7 8 9 10 11
12 13 14 15
16 17 18 19
20 21 22 23
24 25 26 27
28 29 30 31

MONDAY
TUESDAY
WEDNESDAY
THURSDAY
FRIDAY
SATURDAY
SUNDAY

2015
2016
2017
2018
2019
2020
2021
2022
2023
2024
2025
2026
2027
2028
2029

Write Today's Date: _____

START YOUR DAY!

Copy a Verse or Quote:

_____
_____
_____
_____
_____
_____
_____

Draw Your Plans

To-Do List

_____
_____
_____
_____
_____
_____

WORKING DOGS

LOOK AT THE PICTURE AND TRY TO ANSWER THESE QUESTIONS:

What type of job is this?

_____

How many dogs and/or people does it take to perform this job?

_____

What types of dogs can do this job?

_____

What special training and commands are required with this job?

_____

Is there special equipment needed for this job?

_____

What is the role of the dogs human partner in this job?

_____

Picture Study

Look closely at this picture.

Think about the lines and shadows.

Practice working with your colored pencils.

Golden Retriever

DRAW THE MISSING PARTS

Use a variety of smooth black drawing pens, with fine points, to complete the picture.

READING TIME - 1 HOUR (SET A TIMER)

Choose Four Books - Read from each book for 15 minutes.

Copy important words or pictures from each book here:

Spelling Time

Find 20 Words with **4** letters each.
Look in your books for words.
Write the words here:

_____   _____

_____   _____

_____   _____

_____   _____

_____   _____

_____   _____

_____   _____

_____   _____

_____   _____

_____   _____

Start Time:

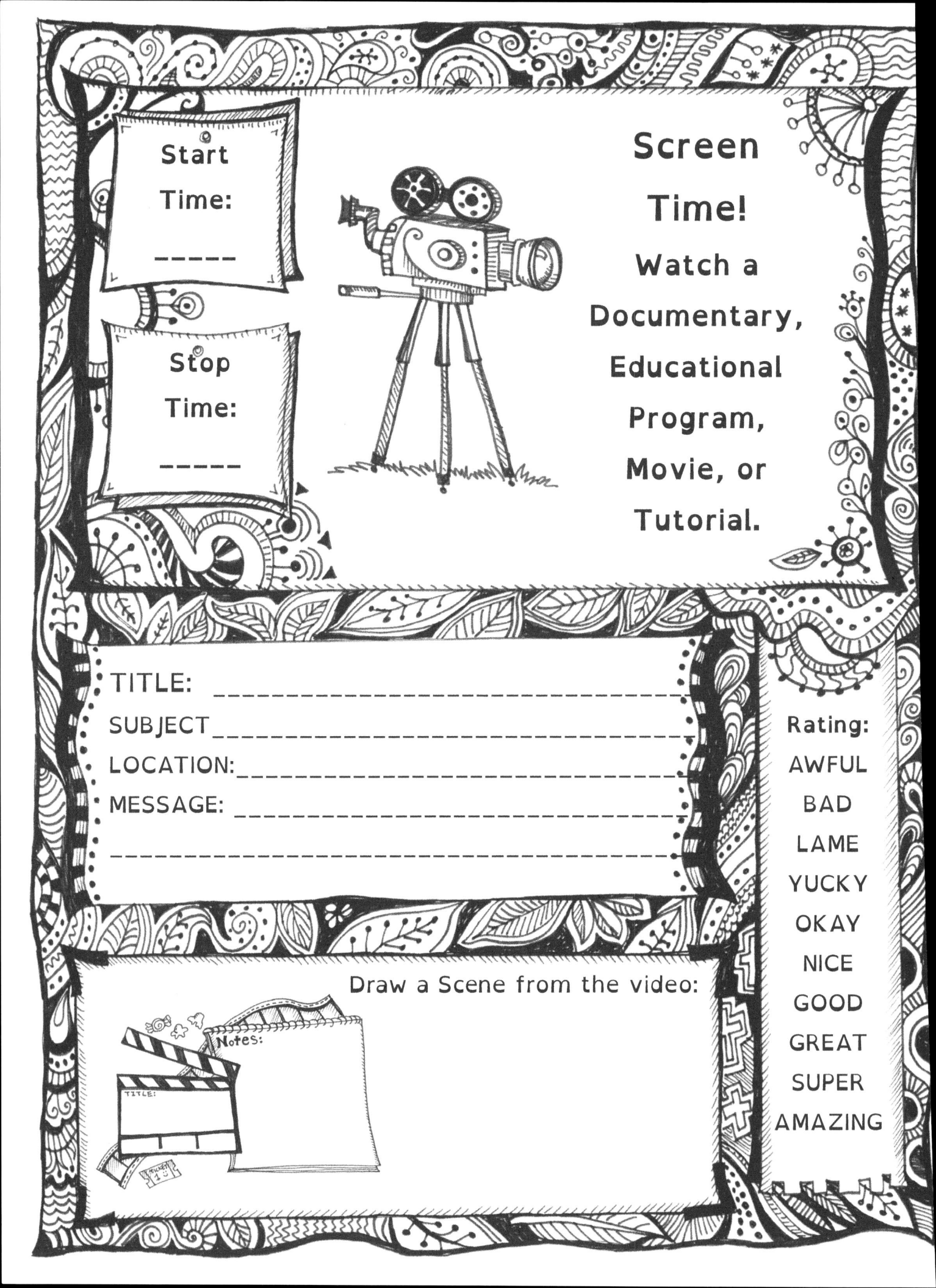

Stop Time:

Screen Time!

Watch a Documentary, Educational Program, Movie, or Tutorial.

TITLE: _____
SUBJECT _____
LOCATION: _____
MESSAGE: _____
_____

Rating:
AWFUL
BAD
LAME
YUCKY
OKAY
NICE
GOOD
GREAT
SUPER
AMAZING

Draw a Scene from the video:

Notes:

Use THIS PAGE for Math Practice
Or be creative and design something, like a dog house!
You could make graphs, maps or geometric designs with this graph paper.

Listening Time

Listen to an audio book or classical music or ask someone to read a story to you while you color and draw on the next page.

What are you listening to?

_____

JUST FOR FUN! FINISH THE PICTURES

CIRCLE TODAY'S DATE

January
February
March
April
May
June
July
August
September
October
November
December

1 2 3 4 5 6
7 8 9 10 11
12 13 14 15
16 17 18 19
20 21 22 23
24 25 26 27
28 29 30 31

MONDAY
TUESDAY
WEDNESDAY
THURSDAY
FRIDAY
SATURDAY
SUNDAY

2015
2016
2017
2018
2019
2020
2021
2022
2023
2024
2025
2026
2027
2028
2029

Write Today's Date:_____

START YOUR DAY!

Copy a Verse or Quote:

_____
_____
_____
_____
_____
_____

Draw Your Plans

To-Do List

_____
_____
_____
_____
_____
_____

WORKING DOGS

LOOK AT THE PICTURE AND TRY TO ANSWER THESE QUESTIONS:

What type of job is this?

_____

How many dogs and/or people does it take to perform this job?

_____

What types of dogs can do this job?

_____

What special training and commands are required with this job?

_____

Is there special equipment needed for this job?

_____

What is the role of the dogs human partner in this job?

_____

WORKING WITH DOGS

CAREERS WITH DOGS

LOOK AT THE PICTURE AND TRY TO ANSWER THESE QUESTIONS:

What type of job is this?
_____

What kind of training does a person need to do this job?
_____

What kinds of dogs are involved in this job?
_____

Is there special equipment needed for this job?
_____

How much money does a person earn for doing this job?
_____

Is this a job you would like to do? Why or why not?
_____
_____
_____
_____
_____
_____
_____
_____

COLOR WITH A FRIEND

SHARE THIS PAGE

READING TIME - 1 HOUR (SET A TIMER)

Choose Four Books - Read from each book for 15 minutes.

Copy important words or pictures from each book here:

Spelling Time

Find 20 Words with **4** letters each.
Look in your books for words.
Write the words here:

_____   _____
_____   _____
_____   _____
_____   _____
_____   _____
_____   _____
_____   _____
_____   _____
_____   _____
_____   _____

Start Time:
_____

Stop Time:
_____

Screen Time!

Watch a Documentary, Educational Program, Movie, or Tutorial.

TITLE: _____
SUBJECT _____
LOCATION: _____
MESSAGE: _____
_____

Rating:
AWFUL
BAD
LAME
YUCKY
OKAY
NICE
GOOD
GREAT
SUPER
AMAZING

Draw a Scene from the video:

Notes:

Use THIS PAGE for Math Practice
Or be creative and design something, like a dog house!
You could make graphs, maps or geometric designs with this graph paper.

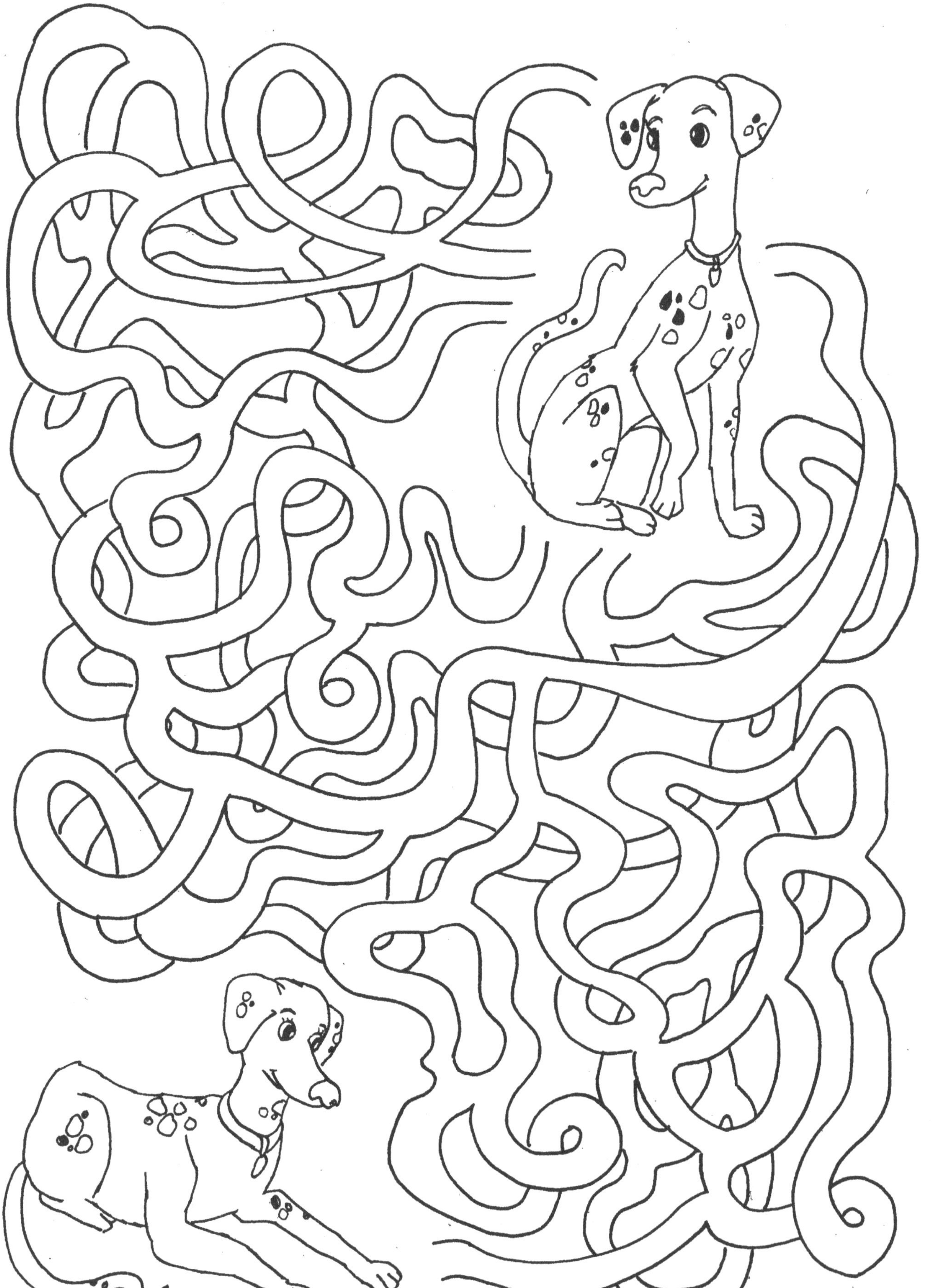

CIRCLE TODAY'S DATE

January
February
March
April
May
June
July
August
September
October
November
December

1 2 3 4 5 6
7 8 9 10 11
12 13 14 15
16 17 18 19
20 21 22 23
24 25 26 27
28 29 30 31

MONDAY
TUESDAY
WEDNESDAY
THURSDAY
FRIDAY
SATURDAY
SUNDAY

2015
2016
2017
2018
2019
2020
2021
2022
2023
2024
2025
2026
2027
2028
2029

Write Today's Date: _ _ _ _ _ _ _ _ _ _ _ _ _

START YOUR DAY!

Copy a Verse or Quote:

_____
_____
_____
_____
_____
_____

Draw Your Plans

To-Do List

_____
_____
_____
_____
_____
_____

WORKING DOGS

LOOK AT THE PICTURE AND TRY TO ANSWER THESE QUESTIONS:

What type of job is this?

_____

How many dogs and/or people does it take to perform this job?

_____

What types of dogs can do this job?

_____

What special training and commands are required with this job?

_____

Is there special equipment needed for this job?

_____

What is the role of the dogs human partner in this job?

_____

WORKING WITH DOGS

CAREERS WITH DOGS

LOOK AT THE PICTURE AND TRY TO ANSWER THESE QUESTIONS:

What type of job is this?

What kind of training does a person need to do this job?

What kinds of dogs are involved in this job?

Is there special equipment needed for this job?

How much money does a person earn for doing this job?

Is this a job you would like to do? Why or why not?

READING TIME - 1 HOUR (SET A TIMER)

Choose Four Books - Read from each book for 15 minutes.

Copy important words or pictures from each book here:

Spelling Time

Find 20 Words with 4 letters each.
Look in your books for words.
Write the words here:

_____   _____

_____   _____

_____   _____

_____   _____

_____   _____

_____   _____

_____   _____

_____   _____

_____   _____

_____   _____

Start Time:
_____

Stop Time:
_____

Screen Time!

Watch a Documentary, Educational Program, Movie, or Tutorial.

TITLE: _____
SUBJECT _____
LOCATION: _____
MESSAGE: _____
_____

Rating:
AWFUL
BAD
LAME
YUCKY
OKAY
NICE
GOOD
GREAT
SUPER
AMAZING

Draw a Scene from the video:

Notes:
TITLE:

Use THIS PAGE for Math Practice
Or be creative and design something, like a dog house!
You could make graphs, maps or geometric designs with this graph paper.

CHOOSE A DOG BREED:

Where does this breed originally come from?
_____
_____

What are some special traits specific to this breed?
_____
_____

Are there any famous dogs that were this breed?
_____
_____

What else did you find out?
_____
_____

DRAW THE BREED:

DOGS IN HISTORY!
ADD CLIP ART, DRAWINGS, PICTURES OR PHOTOS

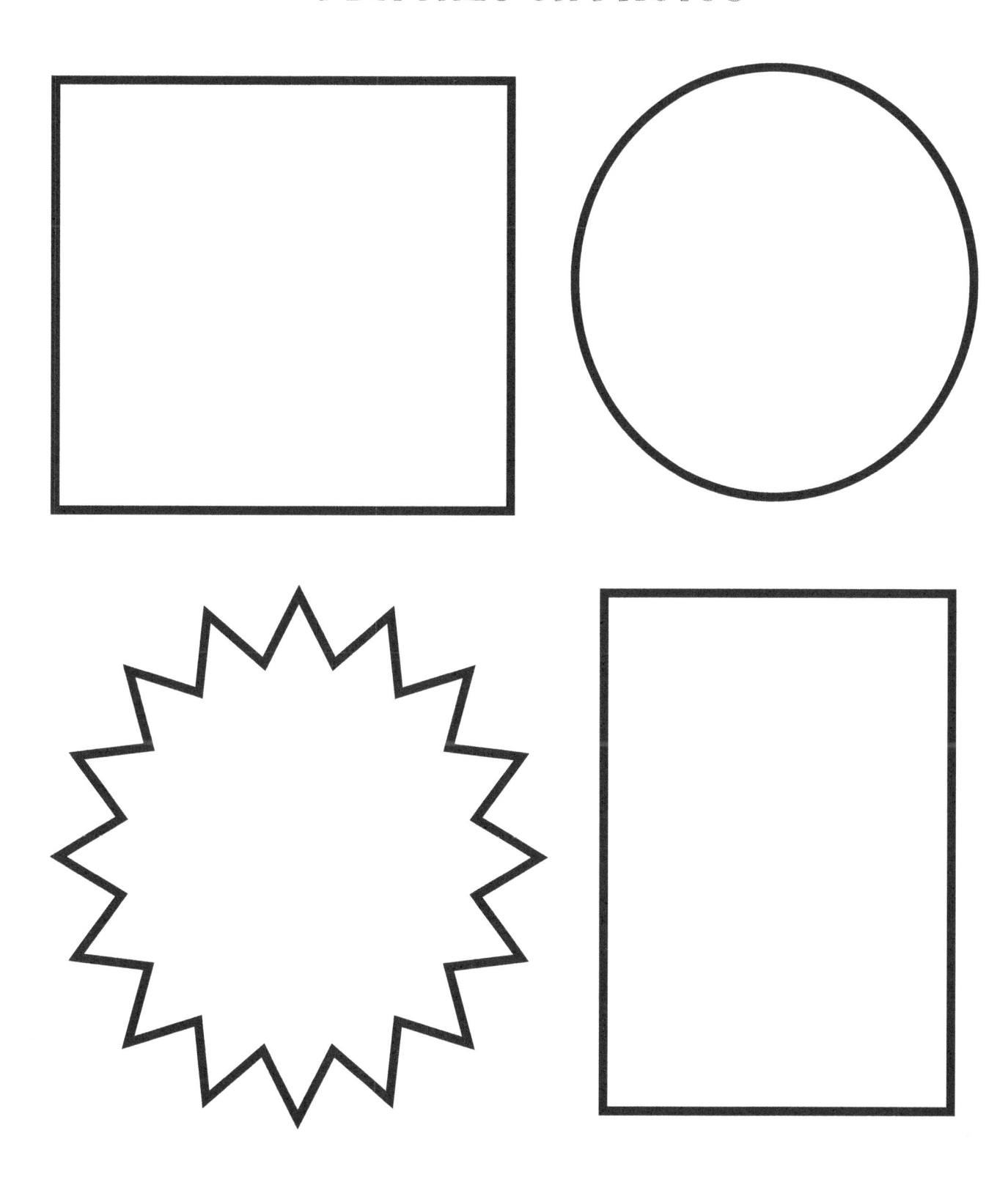

CIRCLE TODAY'S DATE

January
February
March
April
May
June
July
August
September
October
November
December

1 2 3 4 5 6
7 8 9 10 11
12 13 14 15
16 17 18 19
20 21 22 23
24 25 26 27
28 29 30 31

MONDAY
TUESDAY
WEDNESDAY
THURSDAY
FRIDAY
SATURDAY
SUNDAY

2015
2016
2017
2018
2019
2020
2021
2022
2023
2024
2025
2026
2027
2028
2029

Write Today's Date: _ _ _ _ _ _ _ _ _ _ _ _ _ _

START YOUR DAY!

Copy a Verse or Quote:

_____
_____
_____
_____
_____
_____

Draw Your Plans

To-Do List

_____
_____
_____
_____
_____
_____

THE DOG SHOP!
YOU HAVE $12.50 TO SPEND ON YOUR DOG!

Color the items you will buy
Use a calculator to add up your purchase: $_____
How much change will you receive? $_____

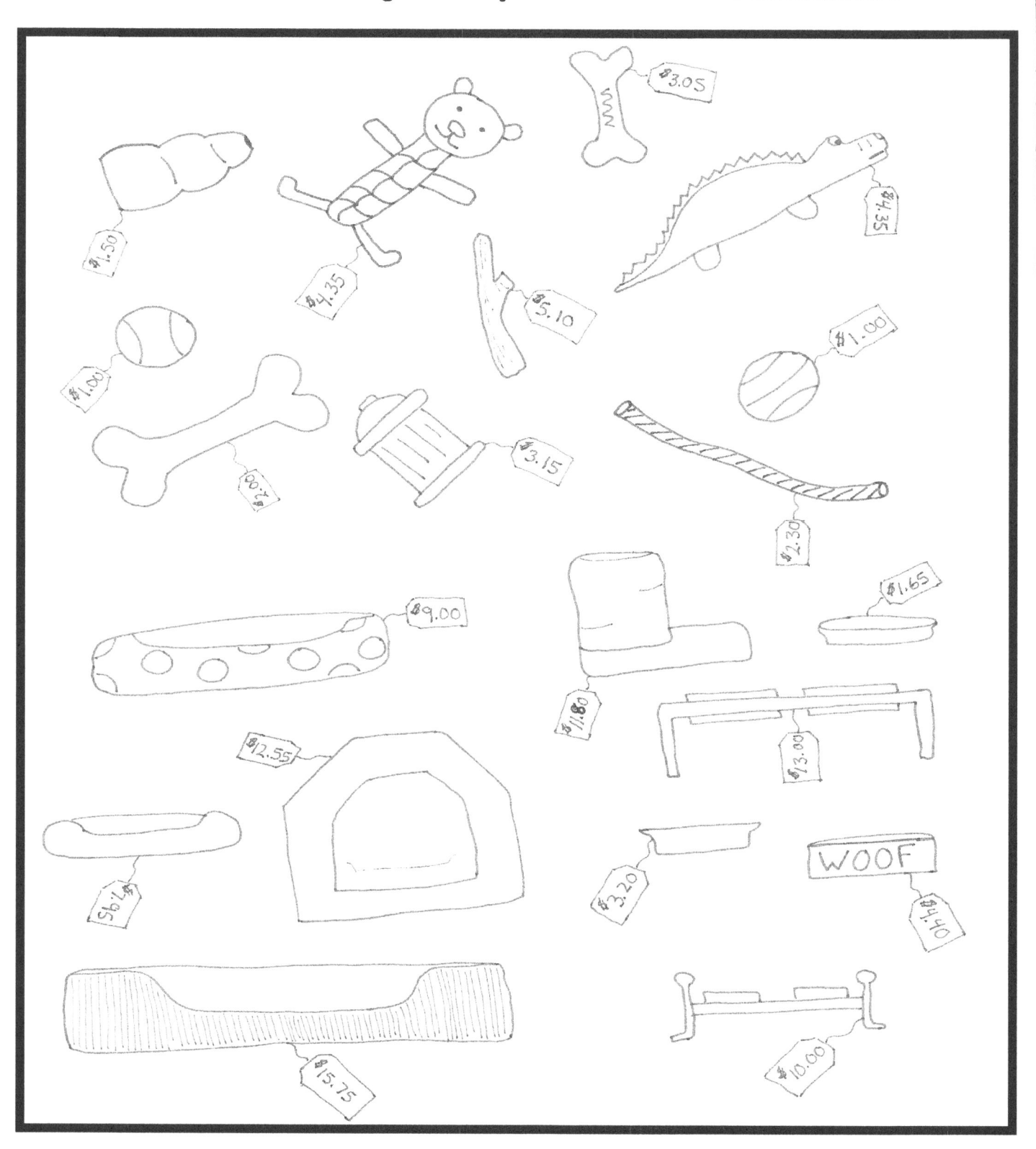

COMPLETE THE COMIC! WHAT HAPPENS NEXT?

Picture Study

Look closely at this picture.

Think about the lines and shadows.

Practice working with your colored pencils.

Saint Bernard

DRAW THE MISSING PARTS

Use a variety of smooth black drawing pens, with fine points, to complete the picture.

WORKING DOGS

LOOK AT THE PICTURE AND TRY TO ANSWER THESE QUESTIONS:

What type of job is this?

_____

How many dogs and/or people does it take to perform this job?

_____

What types of dogs can do this job?

_____

What special training and commands are required with this job?

_____

Is there special equipment needed for this job?

_____

What is the role of the dogs human partner in this job?

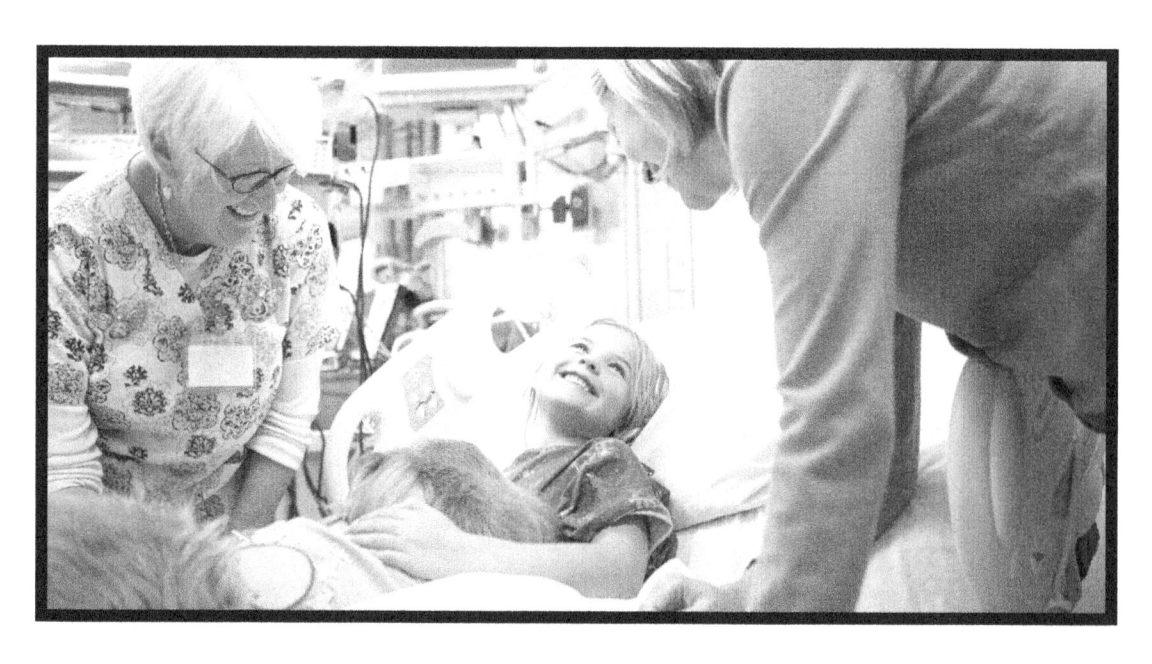

_____

READING TIME - 1 HOUR (SET A TIMER)

Choose Four Books - Read from each book for 15 minutes.

Copy important words or pictures from each book here:

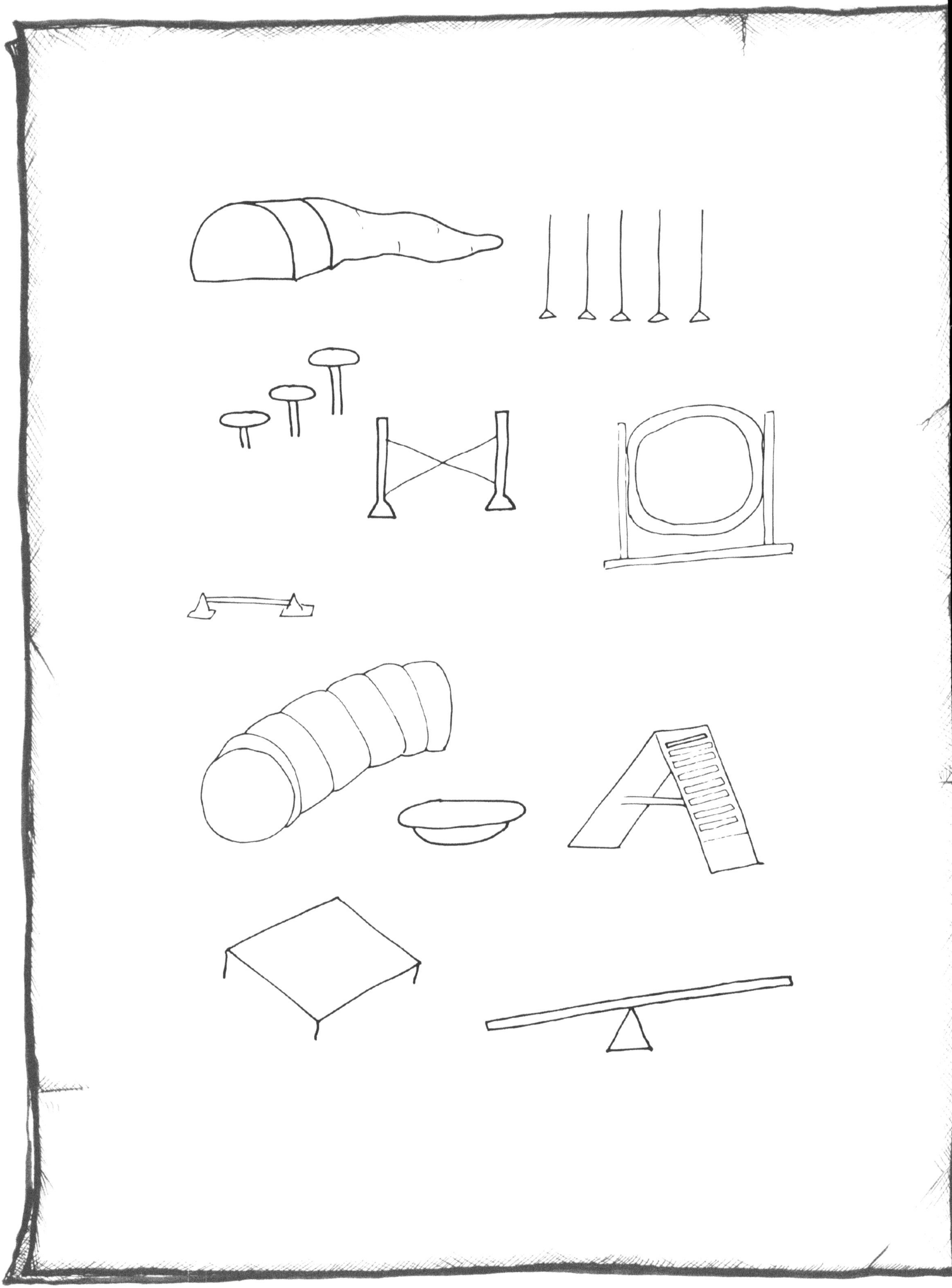

Start Time:
_____

Stop Time:
_____

Screen Time!

Watch a Documentary, Educational Program, Movie, or Tutorial.

TITLE: _____
SUBJECT _____
LOCATION: _____
MESSAGE: _____
_____

Rating:
AWFUL
BAD
LAME
YUCKY
OKAY
NICE
GOOD
GREAT
SUPER
AMAZING

Draw a Scene from the video:

Notes:

Use THIS PAGE for Math Practice
Or be creative and design something, like a dog house!
You could make graphs, maps or geometric designs with this graph paper.

CIRCLE TODAY'S DATE

January
February
March
April
May
June
July
August
September
October
November
December

1 2 3 4 5 6
7 8 9 10 11
12 13 14 15
16 17 18 19
20 21 22 23
24 25 26 27
28 29 30 31

MONDAY
TUESDAY
WEDNESDAY
THURSDAY
FRIDAY
SATURDAY
SUNDAY

2015
2016
2017
2018
2019
2020
2021
2022
2023
2024
2025
2026
2027
2028
2029

Write Today's Date: _ _ _ _ _ _ _ _ _ _ _ _ _

START YOUR DAY!

Copy a Verse or Quote:

_____
_____
_____
_____
_____
_____
_____

Draw Your Plans

To-Do List

_____
_____
_____
_____
_____
_____

WORKING DOGS

LOOK AT THE PICTURE AND TRY TO ANSWER THESE QUESTIONS:

What type of job is this?

_____

How many dogs and/or people does it take to perform this job?

_____

What types of dogs can do this job?

_____

What special training and commands are required with this job?

_____

Is there special equipment needed for this job?

_____

What is the role of the dogs human partner in this job?

_____

Picture Study

Look closely at this picture.
Think about the lines and shadows.
Practice working with your colored pencils.

lhasa Apso

Picture Study

Look closely at this picture.

Think about the lines and shadows.

Practice working with your colored pencils.

READING TIME - 1 HOUR (SET A TIMER)

Choose Four Books - Read from each book for 15 minutes.

Copy important words or pictures from each book here:

Spelling Time

Find 20 Words with 6 letters each.
Look in your books for words.
Write the words here:

_____   _____

_____   _____

_____   _____

_____   _____

_____   _____

_____   _____

_____   _____

_____   _____

_____   _____

_____   _____

Start Time: _____

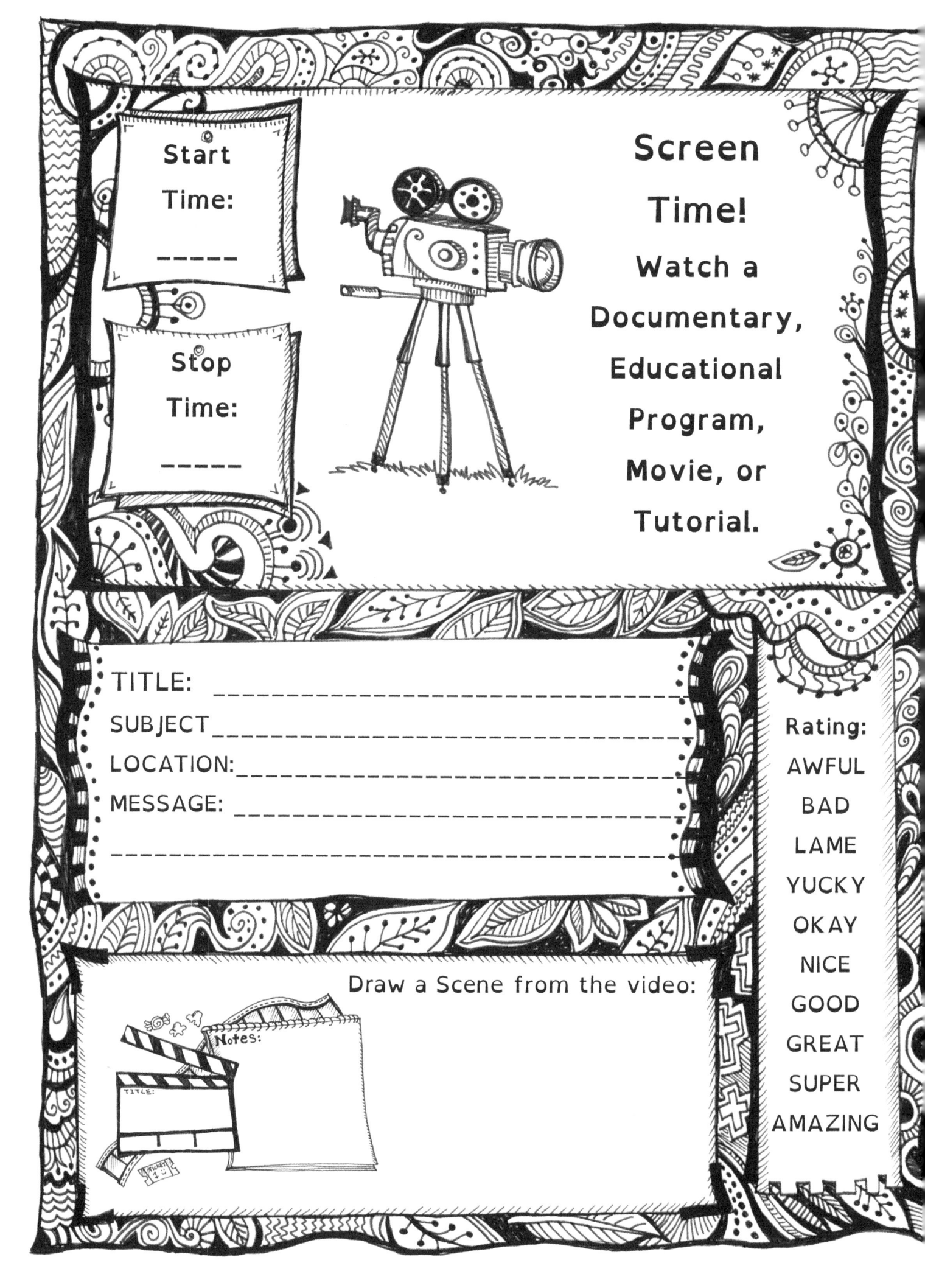

Stop Time: _____

Screen Time!

Watch a Documentary, Educational Program, Movie, or Tutorial.

TITLE: _____
SUBJECT _____
LOCATION: _____
MESSAGE: _____
_____

Rating:
AWFUL
BAD
LAME
YUCKY
OKAY
NICE
GOOD
GREAT
SUPER
AMAZING

Draw a Scene from the video:

Notes:

TITLE:

Use THIS PAGE for Math Practice
Or be creative and design something, like a dog house!
You could make graphs, maps or geometric designs with this graph paper.

World News Today!

Talk to your parents about current events.

Look at a newspaper, news broadcast or website.

Color the countries you learn about.

Tell the news stories with words or pictures.

START YOUR DAY!

Copy a Verse or Quote:
_____
_____
_____
_____
_____
_____
_____

Draw Your Plans

To-Do List
_____
_____
_____
_____
_____

Picture Study

Look closely at this picture.

Think about the lines and shadows.

Practice working with your colored pencils.

Jack Russel

DRAW THE MISSING PARTS

Use a variety of smooth black drawing pens, with fine points, to complete the picture.

JUST FOR FUN!
USE YOUR IMAGINATION

READING TIME - 1 HOUR (SET A TIMER)

Choose Four Books - Read from each book for 15 minutes.

Copy important words or pictures from each book here:

Spelling Time

Find 20 Words with 7 letters each.
Look in your books for words.
Write the words here:

Start Time: _____

Stop Time: _____

Screen Time!

Watch a Documentary, Educational Program, Movie, or Tutorial.

TITLE: _____
SUBJECT _____
LOCATION: _____
MESSAGE: _____
_____

Rating:
AWFUL
BAD
LAME
YUCKY
OKAY
NICE
GOOD
GREAT
SUPER
AMAZING

Draw a Scene from the video:

Notes:

TITLE:

COLOR WITH A FRIEND

SHARE THIS PAGE

WORKING WITH DOGS

CAREERS WITH DOGS

LOOK AT THE PICTURE AND TRY TO ANSWER THESE QUESTIONS:

What type of job is this?

_____

What kind of training does a person need to do this job?

_____

What kinds of dogs are involved in this job?

_____

Is there special equipment needed for this job?

_____

How much money does a person earn for doing this job?

_____

Is this a job you would like to do? Why or why not?

_____
_____
_____
_____
_____
_____
_____
_____

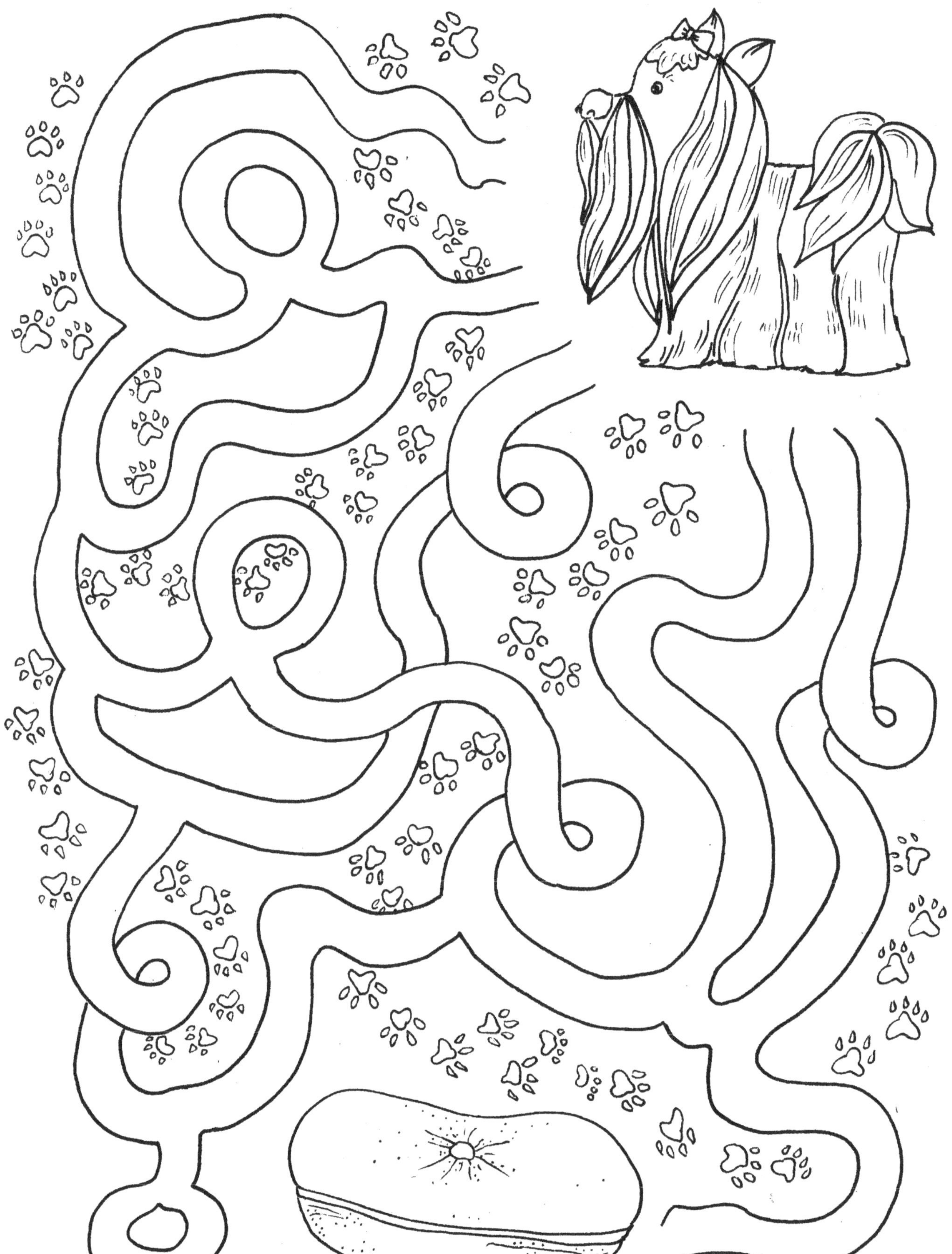

CIRCLE TODAY'S DATE

January
February
March
April
May
June
July
August
September
October
November
December

1 2 3 4 5 6
7 8 9 10 11
12 13 14 15
16 17 18 19
20 21 22 23
24 25 26 27
28 29 30 31

MONDAY
TUESDAY
WEDNESDAY
THURSDAY
FRIDAY
SATURDAY
SUNDAY

2015
2016
2017
2018
2019
2020
2021
2022
2023
2024
2025
2026
2027
2028
2029

Write Today's Date: _____

START YOUR DAY!

Copy a Verse or Quote:

_____
_____
_____
_____
_____
_____
_____

Draw Your Plans

To-Do List

_____
_____
_____
_____
_____
_____

WORKING DOGS

LOOK AT THE PICTURE AND TRY TO ANSWER THESE QUESTIONS:

What type of job is this?

_____

How many dogs and/or people does it take to perform this job?

_____

What types of dogs can do this job?

_____

What special training and commands are required with this job?

_____

Is there special equipment needed for this job?

_____

What is the role of the dogs human partner in this job?

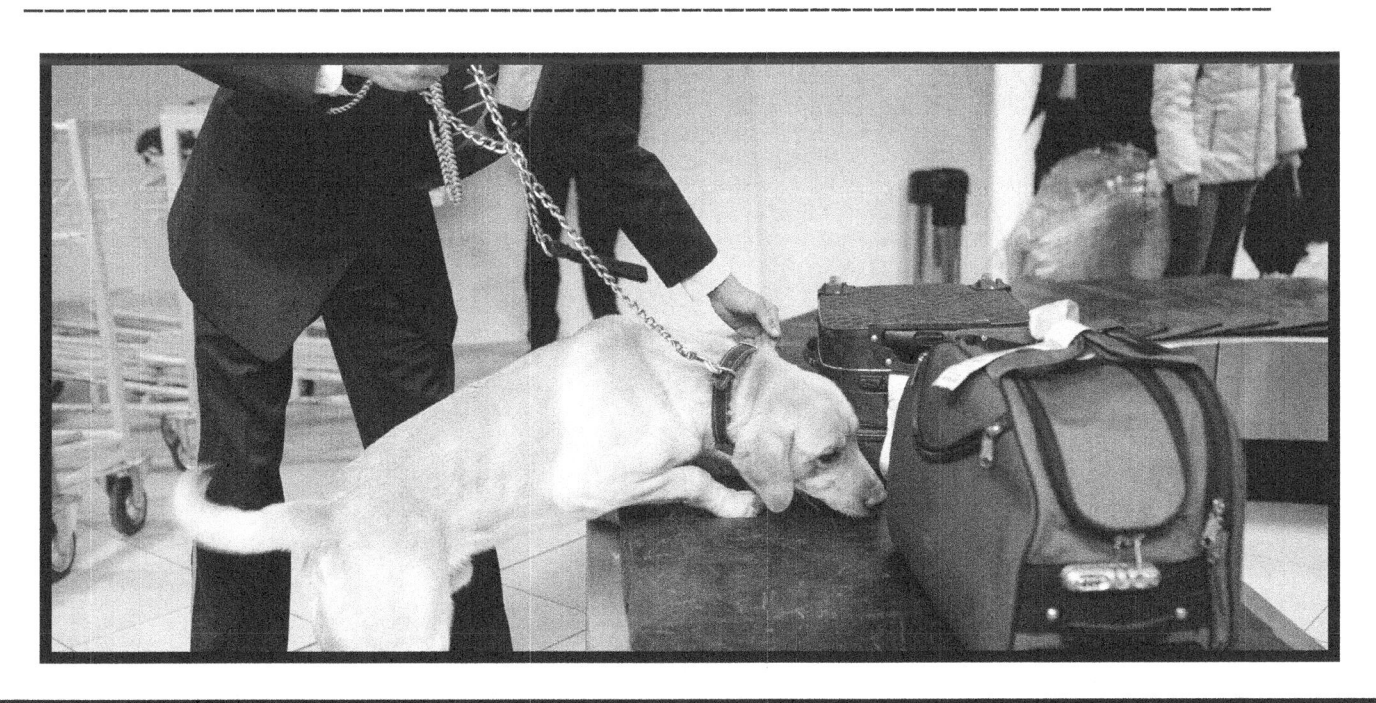

_____

Picture Study

Look closely at this picture.

Think about the lines and shadows.

Practice working with your colored pencils.

Neapolitan Mastiff

DRAW THE MISSING PARTS

Use a variety of smooth black drawing pens, with fine points, to complete the picture.

READING TIME - 1 HOUR (SET A TIMER)

Choose Four Books - Read from each book for 15 minutes.

Copy important words or pictures from each book here:

COMPLETE THE COMIC! WHAT HAPPENS NEXT?

Listening Time

Listen to an audio book or classical music or ask someone to read a story to you while you color and draw on the next page.

What are you listening to?

_____

CIRCLE TODAY'S DATE

January
February
March
April
May
June
July
August
September
October
November
December

1 2 3 4 5 6
7 8 9 10 11
12 13 14 15
16 17 18 19
20 21 22 23
24 25 26 27
28 29 30 31

MONDAY
TUESDAY
WEDNESDAY
THURSDAY
FRIDAY
SATURDAY
SUNDAY

2015
2016
2017
2018
2019
2020
2021
2022
2023
2024
2025
2026
2027
2028
2029

Write Today's Date: _____

START YOUR DAY!

Copy a Verse or Quote:

_____
_____
_____
_____
_____
_____

Draw Your Plans

To-Do List
_____
_____
_____
_____
_____
_____

DRAW YOUR FAVORITE DOG!

Picture Study

Look closely at this picture.

Think about the lines and shadows.

Practice working with your colored pencils.

New Foundland

DRAW THE MISSING PARTS

Use a variety of smooth black drawing pens, with fine points, to complete the picture.

READING TIME - 1 HOUR (SET A TIMER)

Choose Four Books - Read from each book for 15 minutes.

Copy important words or pictures from each book here:

Use THIS PAGE for Math Practice
Or be creative and design something, like a dog house!
You could make graphs, maps or geometric designs with this graph paper.

WORKING WITH DOGS

CIRCLE TODAY'S DATE

January
February
March
April
May
June
July
August
September
October
November
December

1 2 3 4 5 6
7 8 9 10 11
12 13 14 15
16 17 18 19
20 21 22 23
24 25 26 27
28 29 30 31

MONDAY
TUESDAY
WEDNESDAY
THURSDAY
FRIDAY
SATURDAY
SUNDAY

2015
2016
2017
2018
2019
2020
2021
2022
2023
2024
2025
2026
2027
2028
2029

Write Today's Date: _ _ _ _ _ _ _ _ _ _ _ _ _ _ _ _

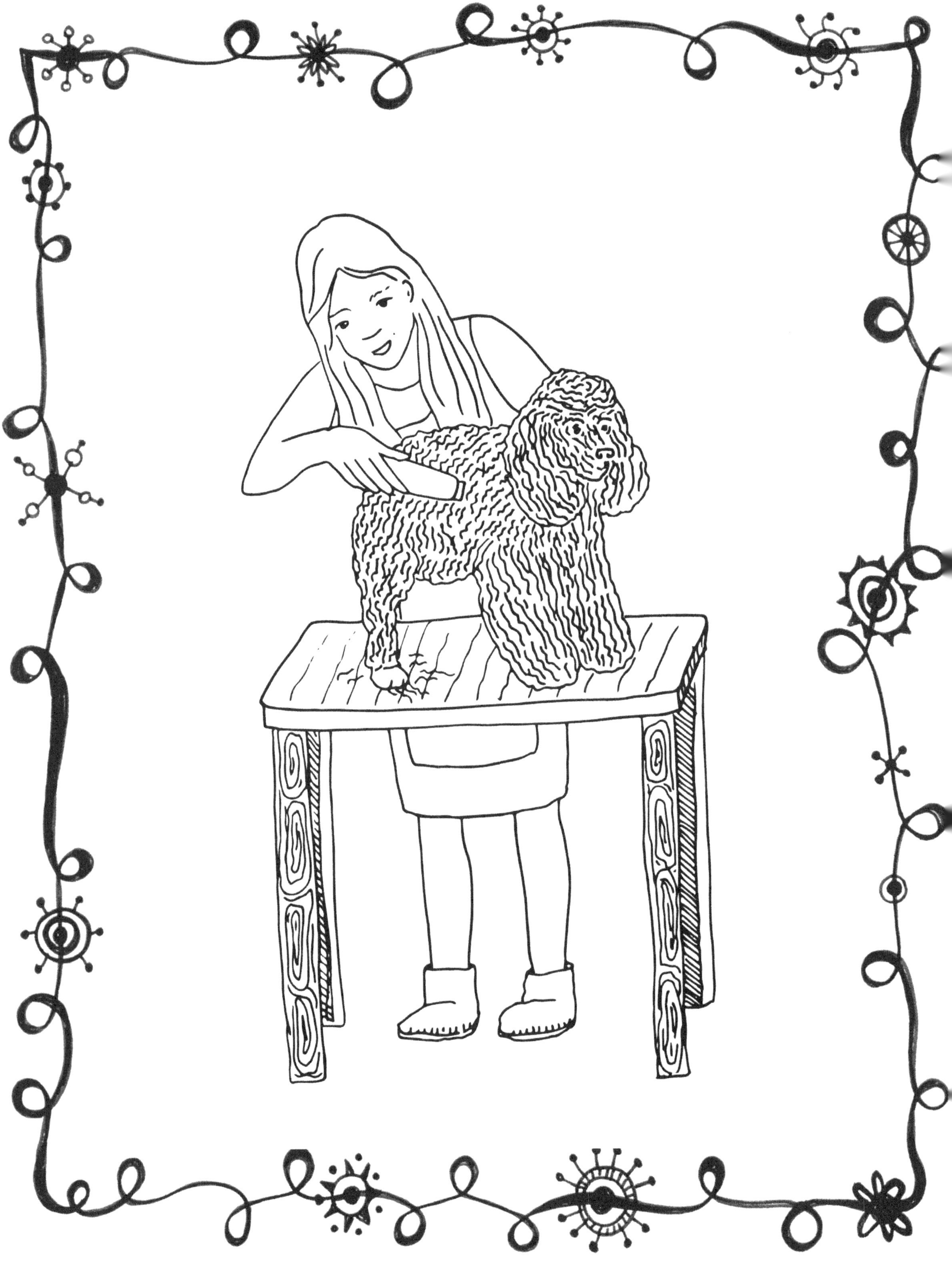

START YOUR DAY!

Copy a Verse or Quote:

_____
_____
_____
_____
_____
_____
_____

Draw Your Plans

To-Do List

_____
_____
_____
_____
_____

Picture Study

Look closely at this picture.

Think about the lines and shadows.

Practice working with your colored pencils.

Pekingese

DRAW THE MISSING PARTS

Use a variety of smooth black drawing pens, with fine points, to complete the picture.

FINISH THE PICTURE!

READING TIME - 1 HOUR (SET A TIMER)

Choose Four Books - Read from each book for 15 minutes.

Copy important words or pictures from each book here:

Spelling Time

Find 20 Words with **8** letters each.
Look in your books for words.
Write the words here:

_____ _____

_____ _____

_____ _____

_____ _____

_____ _____

_____ _____

_____ _____

_____ _____

_____ _____

_____ _____

Start Time:
_____

Stop Time:
_____

Screen Time!

Watch a Documentary, Educational Program, Movie, or Tutorial.

TITLE: _____
SUBJECT _____
LOCATION: _____
MESSAGE: _____
_____

Rating:
AWFUL
BAD
LAME
YUCKY
OKAY
NICE
GOOD
GREAT
SUPER
AMAZING

Draw a Scene from the video:

Notes:

TITLE:

Use THIS PAGE for Math Practice
Or be creative and design something, like a dog house!
You could make graphs, maps or geometric designs with this graph paper.

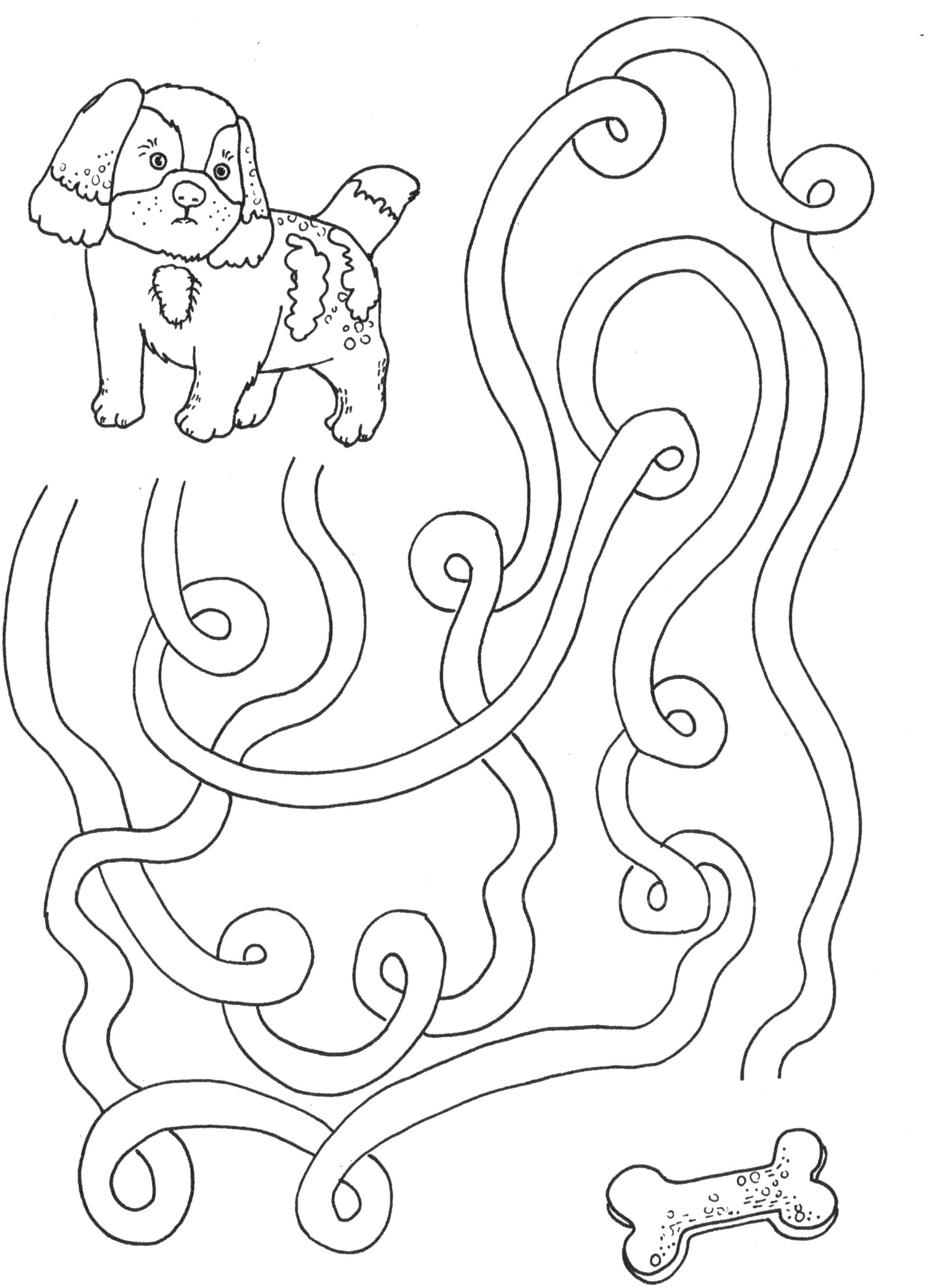

CIRCLE TODAY'S DATE

January
February
March
April
May
June
July
August
September
October
November
December

1 2 3 4 5 6
7 8 9 10 11
12 13 14 15
16 17 18 19
20 21 22 23
24 25 26 27
28 29 30 31

MONDAY
TUESDAY
WEDNESDAY
THURSDAY
FRIDAY
SATURDAY
SUNDAY

2015
2016
2017
2018
2019
2020
2021
2022
2023
2024
2025
2026
2027
2028
2029

Write Today's Date: _ _ _ _ _ _ _ _ _ _ _ _ _

START YOUR DAY!

Copy a Verse or Quote:
_____
_____
_____
_____
_____
_____

Draw Your Plans

To-Do List
_____
_____
_____
_____
_____

Picture Study

Look closely at this picture.

Think about the lines and shadows.

Practice working with your colored pencils.

Pit-bull

DRAW THE MISSING PARTS

Use a variety of smooth black drawing pens, with fine points, to complete the picture.

My FUN Page

READING TIME - 1 HOUR (SET A TIMER)

Choose Four Books - Read from each book for 15 minutes.

Copy important words or pictures from each book here:

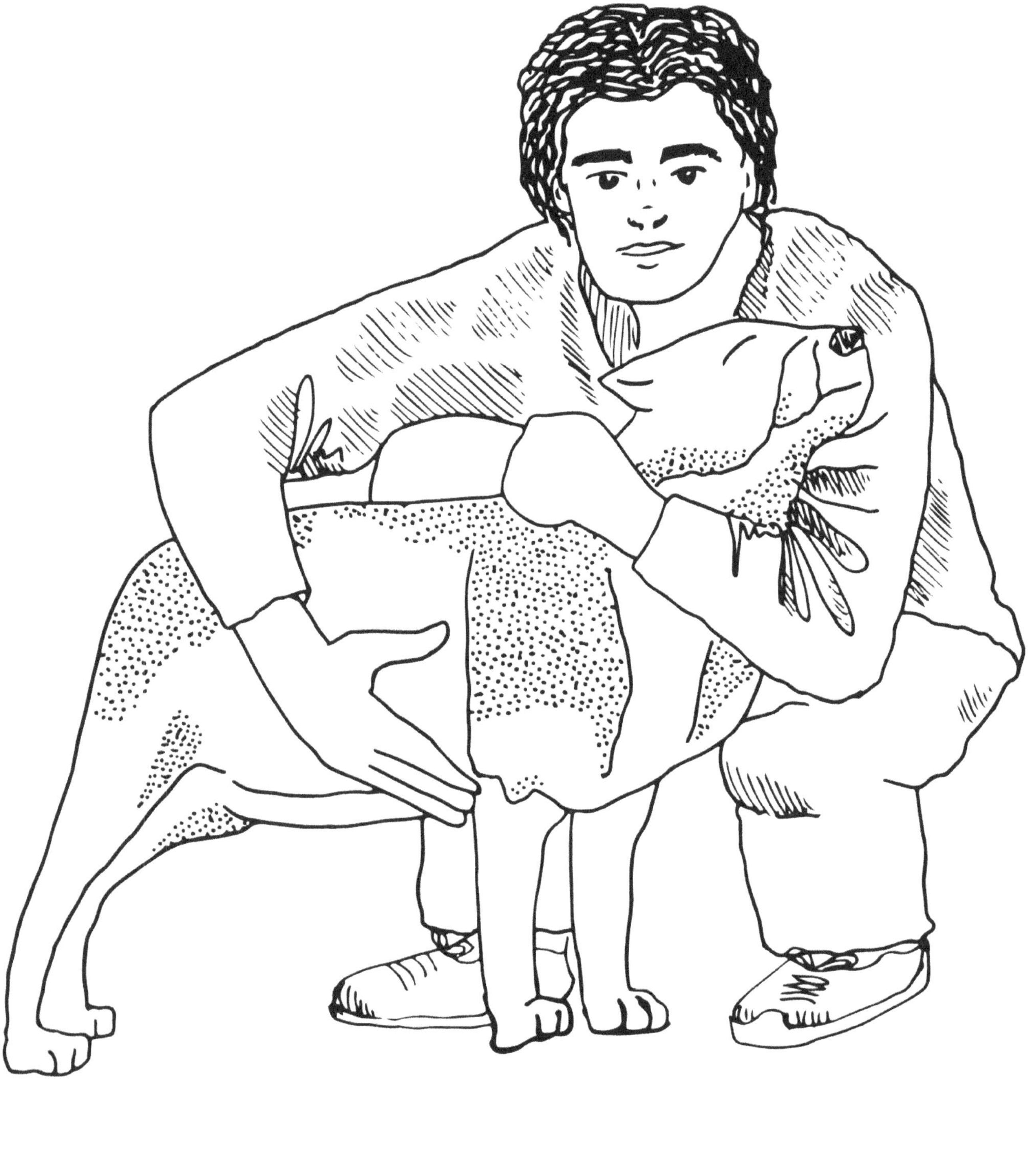

Start Time:

Stop Time:

Screen Time!

Watch a Documentary, Educational Program, Movie, or Tutorial.

TITLE: _____
SUBJECT _____
LOCATION: _____
MESSAGE: _____
_____

Rating:
AWFUL
BAD
LAME
YUCKY
OKAY
NICE
GOOD
GREAT
SUPER
AMAZING

Draw a Scene from the video:

Notes:

TITLE:

THE DOG SHOP!
YOU HAVE $23.10 TO SPEND ON YOUR DOG!

Color the items you will buy
Use a calculator to add up your purchase: $_____
How much change will you receive? $_____

COMPLETE THE COMIC! WHAT HAPPENS NEXT?

COLOR WITH A FRIEND

COPY A PICTURE FROM ONE OF YOUR BOOKS

CIRCLE TODAY'S DATE

January
February
March
April
May
June
July
August
September
October
November
December

1 2 3 4 5 6
7 8 9 10 11
12 13 14 15
16 17 18 19
20 21 22 23
24 25 26 27
28 29 30 31

MONDAY
TUESDAY
WEDNESDAY
THURSDAY
FRIDAY
SATURDAY
SUNDAY

2015
2016
2017
2018
2019
2020
2021
2022
2023
2024
2025
2026
2027
2028
2029

Write Today's Date: _ _ _ _ _ _ _ _ _ _ _ _ _ _ _

START YOUR DAY!

Copy a Verse or Quote:

_____
_____
_____
_____
_____
_____

Draw Your Plans

To-Do List

_____
_____
_____
_____
_____
_____

Picture Study

Look closely at this picture.

Think about the lines and shadows.

Practice working with your colored pencils.

Poodle

DRAW THE MISSING PARTS

Use a variety of smooth black drawing pens, with fine points, to complete the picture.

DRAW A DOG WEARING A COSTUME

Start Time:

Stop Time:

Screen Time!

Watch a Documentary, Educational Program, Movie, or Tutorial.

TITLE: _____
SUBJECT _____
LOCATION: _____
MESSAGE: _____
_____

Rating:
AWFUL
BAD
LAME
YUCKY
OKAY
NICE
GOOD
GREAT
SUPER
AMAZING

Draw a Scene from the video:

Notes:

TITLE:

Use THIS PAGE for Math Practice
Or be creative and design something, like a dog house!
You could make graphs, maps or geometric designs with this graph paper.

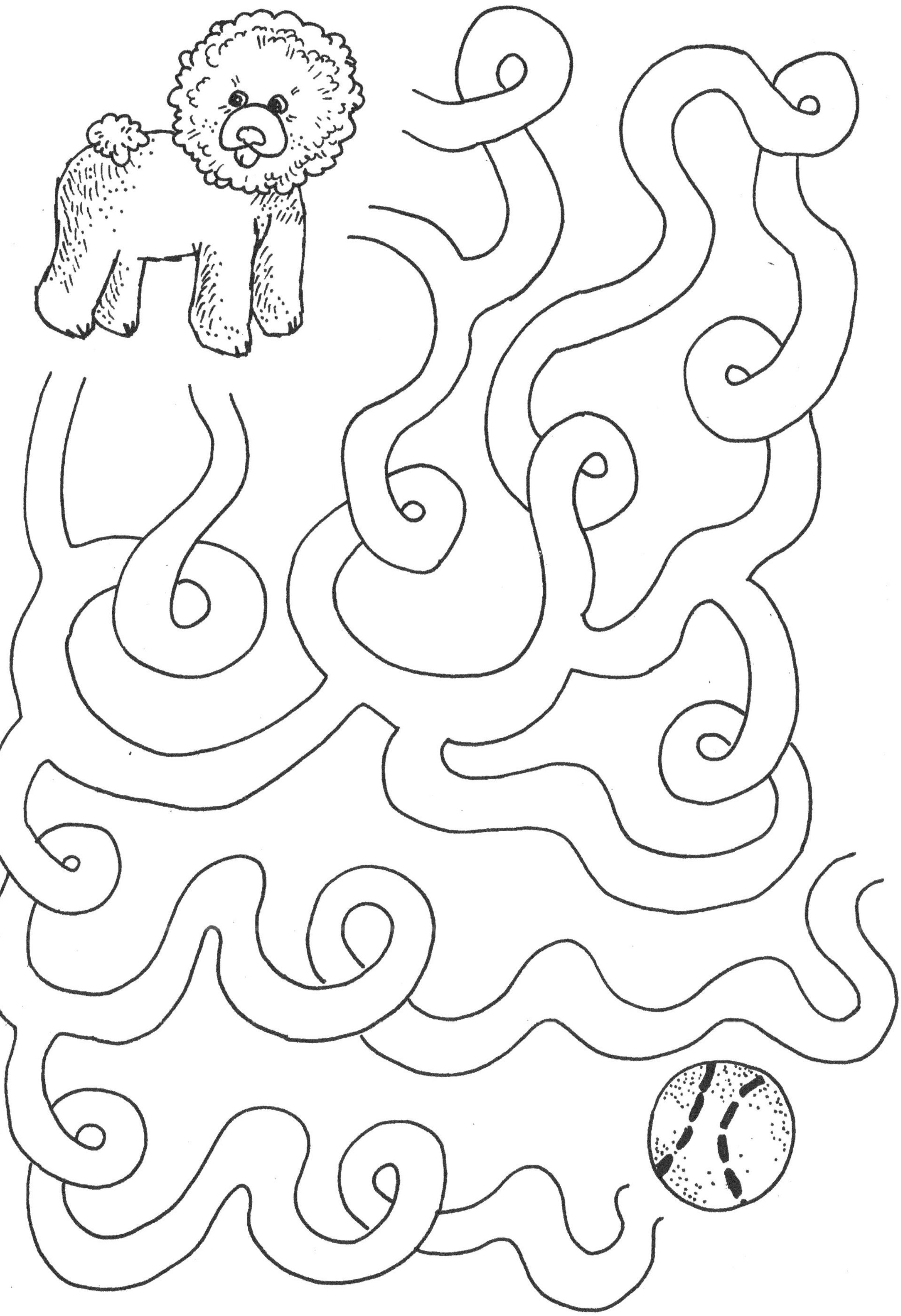

CHOOSE A DOG BREED:

Where does this breed originally come from?
_____
_____

What are some special traits specific to this breed?
_____
_____

Are there any famous dogs that were this breed?
_____
_____

What else did you find out?
_____
_____

DRAW THE BREED:

START YOUR DAY!

Copy a Verse or Quote:

_____
_____
_____
_____
_____
_____
_____

Draw Your Plans

To-Do List

_____
_____
_____
_____
_____
_____

Picture Study

Look closely at this picture.

Think about the lines and shadows.

Practice working with your colored pencils.

Rottweiler

DRAW THE MISSING PARTS

Use a variety of smooth black drawing pens, with fine points, to complete the picture.

DRAW A PICTURE SHOWING THE DIFFERENCES BETWEEN WOLVES, FOXES, AND DOGS.

READING TIME - 1 HOUR (SET A TIMER)

Choose Four Books - Read from each book for 15 minutes.
Copy important words or pictures from each book here:

Spelling Time

Find 20 Words with **6** letters each.
Look in your books for words.
Write the words here:

_____   _____

_____   _____

_____   _____

_____   _____

_____   _____

_____   _____

_____   _____

_____   _____

_____   _____

_____   _____

Start Time: _____

Stop Time: _____

Screen Time!

Watch a Documentary, Educational Program, Movie, or Tutorial.

TITLE: _____
SUBJECT _____
LOCATION: _____
MESSAGE: _____
_____

Rating:
AWFUL
BAD
LAME
YUCKY
OKAY
NICE
GOOD
GREAT
SUPER
AMAZING

Draw a Scene from the video:

Notes:

Use THIS PAGE for Math Practice
Or be creative and design something, like a dog house!
You could make graphs, maps or geometric designs with this graph paper.

CHOOSE A DOG BREED:

Where does this breed originally come from?
_____
_____

What are some special traits specific to this breed?
_____
_____

Are there any famous dogs that were this breed?
_____
_____

What else did you find out?
_____
_____

DRAW THE BREED:

WORKING WITH DOGS

CAREERS WITH DOGS

LOOK AT THE PICTURE AND TRY TO ANSWER THESE QUESTIONS:

What type of job is this?
_____

What kind of training does a person need to do this job?
_____

What kinds of dogs are involved in this job?
_____

Is there special equipment needed for this job?
_____

How much money does a person earn for doing this job?
_____

Is this a job you would like to do? Why or why not?
_____
_____
_____
_____
_____
_____
_____
_____

CIRCLE TODAY'S DATE

January
February
March
April
May
June
July
August
September
October
November
December

1 2 3 4 5 6
7 8 9 10 11
12 13 14 15
16 17 18 19
20 21 22 23
24 25 26 27
28 29 30 31

MONDAY
TUESDAY
WEDNESDAY
THURSDAY
FRIDAY
SATURDAY
SUNDAY

2015
2016
2017
2018
2019
2020
2021
2022
2023
2024
2025
2026
2027
2028
2029

Write Today's Date: _ _ _ _ _ _ _ _ _ _ _ _ _ _ _

START YOUR DAY!

Copy a Verse or Quote:

_____
_____
_____
_____
_____
_____

Draw Your Plans

To-Do List

_____
_____
_____
_____
_____

Picture Study

Look closely at this picture.

Think about the lines and shadows.

Practice working with your colored pencils.

Shar-pei

DRAW THE MISSING PARTS

Use a variety of smooth black drawing pens, with fine points, to complete the picture.

MOTHER DOGS

How long is a dog's gestation period?

_____

How long is a humans?

_____

How long does a mother dog care for her puppies?

_____

Are there similarities in how a dog mother and human mother care for their babies?

_____

_____

_____

Draw a mother dog with her puppies:

READING TIME - 1 HOUR (SET A TIMER)

Choose Four Books - Read from each book for 15 minutes.

Copy important words or pictures from each book here:

Use THIS PAGE for Math Practice
Or be creative and design something, like a dog house!
You could make graphs, maps or geometric designs with this graph paper.

World News Today!

Talk to your parents about current events.

Look at a newspaper, news broadcast or website.

Color the countries you learn about.

Tell the news stories with words or pictures.

FAMOUS DOGS IN THE HISTORY OF THE WORLD

NAME OF DOG:

TYPE OF DOG:

BEST KNOWN FOR:

DATE OF EVENT:

THE STORY OF THIS INTERESTING DOG:

_____
_____
_____
_____
_____
_____
_____
_____
_____
_____

DOGS IN HISTORY!
ADD CLIP ART, DRAWINGS, PICTURES OR PHOTOS

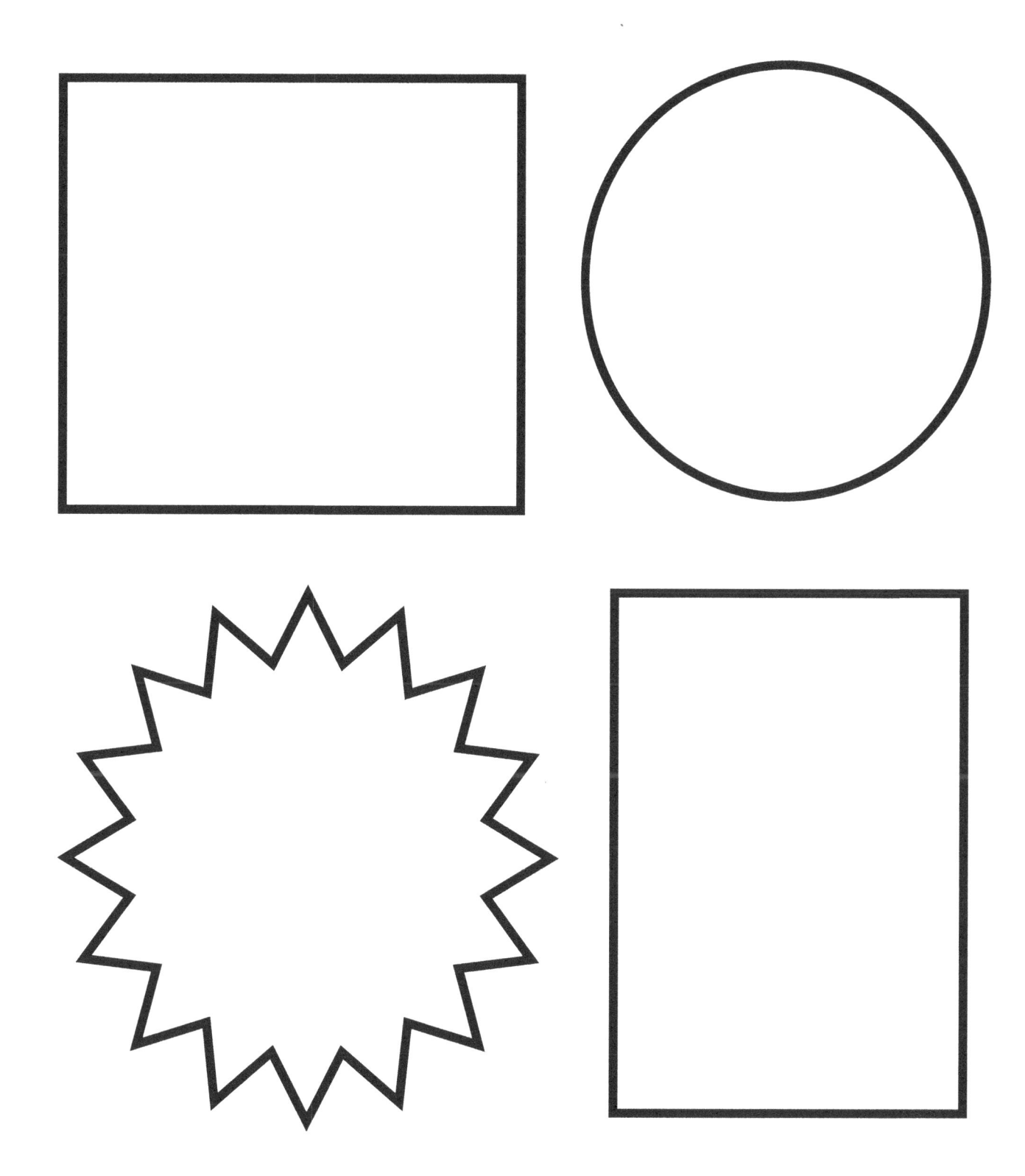

CHOOSE A DOG BREED:

Where does this breed originally come from?
_____
_____

What are some special traits specific to this breed?
_____
_____

Are there any famous dogs that were this breed?
_____
_____

What else did you find out?
_____
_____

DRAW THE BREED:

START YOUR DAY!

Copy a Verse or Quote:

_____
_____
_____
_____
_____
_____
_____

Draw Your Plans

To-Do List

_____
_____
_____
_____
_____
_____

DOG HEALTH

How can you care for your dogs teeth?

Is it different from how you care for your teeth?

Draw a picture of a dog's mouth showing all the teeth:

READING TIME – 1 HOUR (SET A TIMER)

Choose Four Books – Read from each book for 15 minutes.

Copy important words or pictures from each book here:

Spelling Time

Find 20 Words with 6 letters each.
Look in your books for words.
Write the words here:

_____   _____
_____   _____
_____   _____
_____   _____
_____   _____
_____   _____
_____   _____
_____   _____
_____   _____
_____   _____

Start Time:
_____

Stop Time:
_____

Screen Time!

Watch a Documentary, Educational Program, Movie, or Tutorial.

TITLE: _____
SUBJECT _____
LOCATION: _____
MESSAGE: _____
_____

Rating:
AWFUL
BAD
LAME
YUCKY
OKAY
NICE
GOOD
GREAT
SUPER
AMAZING

Draw a Scene from the video:

Notes:

TITLE:

Use THIS PAGE for Math Practice
Or be creative and design something, like a dog house!
You could make graphs, maps or geometric designs with this graph paper.

CAREERS WITH DOGS

LOOK AT THE PICTURE AND TRY TO ANSWER THESE QUESTIONS:

What type of job is this?

_____

What kind of training does a person need to do this job?

_____

What kinds of dogs are involved in this job?

_____

Is there special equipment needed for this job?

_____

How much money does a person earn for doing this job?

_____

Is this a job you would like to do? Why or why not?

_____
_____
_____
_____
_____
_____
_____
_____

COLOR WITH A FRIEND

SHARE THIS PAGE

CIRCLE TODAY'S DATE

January February March April May June July August September October November December	1 2 3 4 5 6 7 8 9 10 11 12 13 14 15 16 17 18 19 20 21 22 23 24 25 26 27 28 29 30 31
MONDAY TUESDAY WEDNESDAY THURSDAY FRIDAY SATURDAY SUNDAY	2015 2016 2017 2018 2019 2020 2021 2022 2023 2024 2025 2026 2027 2028 2029

Write Today's Date: _____

START YOUR DAY!

Copy a Verse or Quote:

_____
_____
_____
_____
_____
_____
_____

Draw Your Plans

To-Do List

_____
_____
_____
_____
_____
_____

Picture Study

Look closely at this picture.

Think about the lines and shadows.

Practice working with your colored pencils.

Shetland Sheep Dog

DRAW THE MISSING PARTS

Use a variety of smooth black drawing pens, with fine points, to complete the picture.

CAN YOU DRAW THE BONES IN A DOGS PAW?

CAN YOU DRAW A DOG'S PAW PRINTS?

READING TIME - 1 HOUR (SET A TIMER)

Choose Four Books - Read from each book for 15 minutes.

Copy important words or pictures from each book here:

Spelling Time

Find 20 Words with 7 letters each.
Look in your books for words.
Write the words here:

_____   _____

_____   _____

_____   _____

_____   _____

_____   _____

_____   _____

_____   _____

_____   _____

_____   _____

_____   _____

Start Time: _____

Stop Time: _____

Screen Time!

Watch a Documentary, Educational Program, Movie, or Tutorial.

TITLE: _____
SUBJECT _____
LOCATION: _____
MESSAGE: _____
_____

Rating:
AWFUL
BAD
LAME
YUCKY
OKAY
NICE
GOOD
GREAT
SUPER
AMAZING

Draw a Scene from the video:

Notes:

WORKING WITH DOGS

CAREERS WITH DOGS

LOOK AT THE PICTURE AND TRY TO ANSWER THESE QUESTIONS:

What type of job is this?

_____

What kind of training does a person need to do this job?

_____

What kinds of dogs are involved in this job?

_____

Is there special equipment needed for this job?

_____

How much money does a person earn for doing this job?

_____

Is this a job you would like to do? Why or why not?

_____
_____
_____
_____
_____
_____
_____
_____
_____

CHOOSE A DOG BREED:

Where does this breed originally come from?
_____
_____

What are some special traits specific to this breed?
_____
_____

Are there any famous dogs that were this breed?
_____
_____

What else did you find out?
_____
_____

DRAW THE BREED:

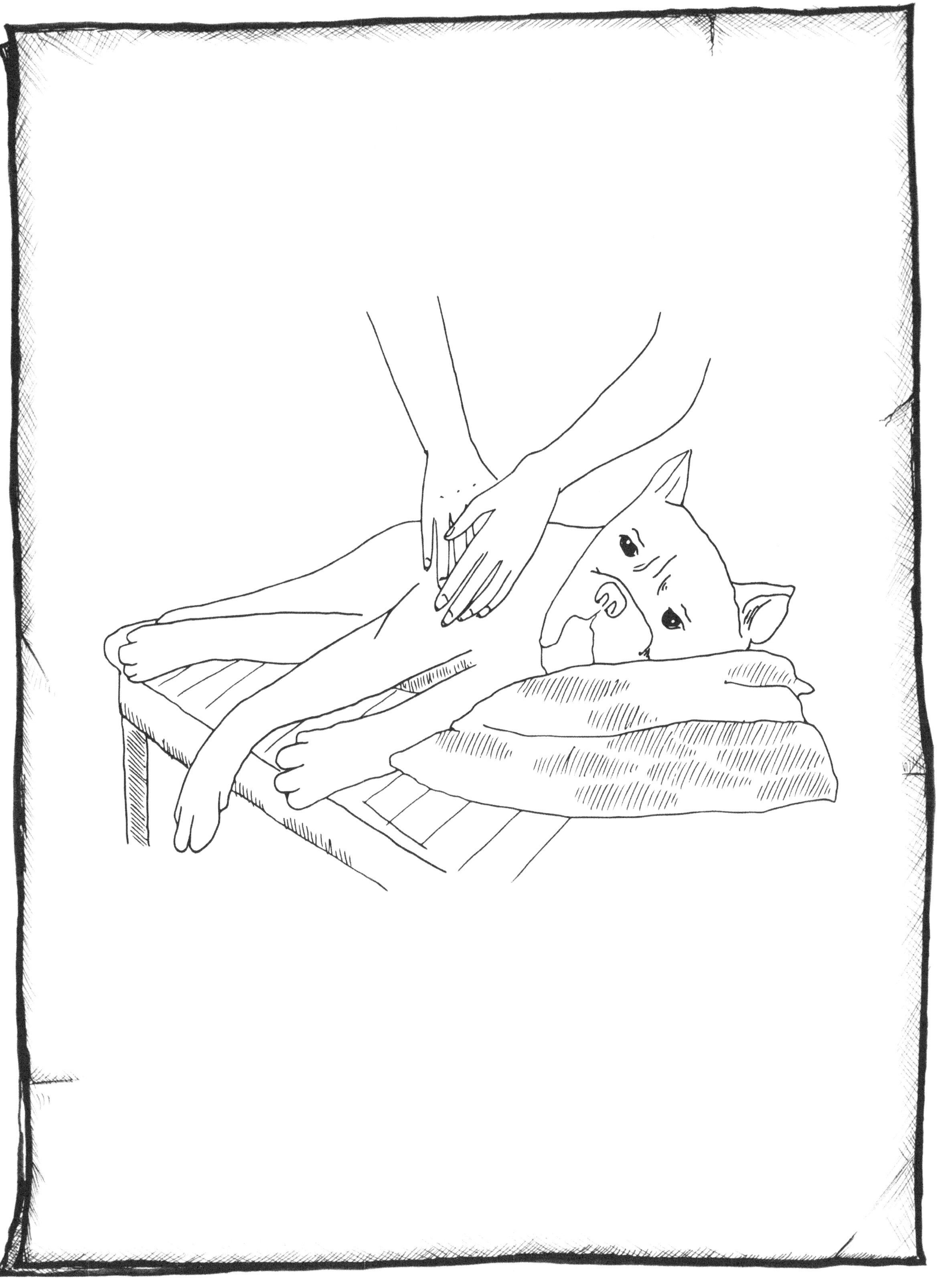

CIRCLE TODAY'S DATE

January
February
March
April
May
June
July
August
September
October
November
December

1 2 3 4 5 6
7 8 9 10 11
12 13 14 15
16 17 18 19
20 21 22 23
24 25 26 27
28 29 30 31

MONDAY
TUESDAY
WEDNESDAY
THURSDAY
FRIDAY
SATURDAY
SUNDAY

2015
2016
2017
2018
2019
2020
2021
2022
2023
2024
2025
2026
2027
2028
2029

Write Today's Date: _____

START YOUR DAY!

Copy a Verse or Quote:

_____
_____
_____
_____
_____
_____
_____

Draw Your Plans

To-Do List

_____
_____
_____
_____
_____
_____

HOW DO YOU CARE FOR A SICK DOG?

_____
_____
_____
_____
_____
_____

HOW IS IT DIFFERENT FROM WHEN YOU ARE SICK?

_____
_____
_____
_____
_____
_____

READING TIME - 1 HOUR (SET A TIMER)

Choose Four Books - Read from each book for 15 minutes.

Copy important words or pictures from each book here:

Picture Study

Look closely at this picture.
Think about the lines and shadows.
Practice working with your colored pencils.

Shih-tsu

DRAW THE MISSING PARTS

Use a variety of smooth black drawing pens, with fine points, to complete the picture.

Spelling Time

Find 20 Words with 8 letters each.
Look in your books for words.
Write the words here:

_____   _____

_____   _____

_____   _____

_____   _____

_____   _____

_____   _____

_____   _____

_____   _____

_____   _____

_____   _____

Start Time:
_____

Stop Time:
_____

Screen Time!

Watch a Documentary, Educational Program, Movie, or Tutorial.

TITLE: _____
SUBJECT _____
LOCATION: _____
MESSAGE: _____
_____

Rating:
AWFUL
BAD
LAME
YUCKY
OKAY
NICE
GOOD
GREAT
SUPER
AMAZING

Draw a Scene from the video:

Notes:

TITLE:

Use THIS PAGE for Math Practice
Or be creative and design something, like a dog house!
You could make graphs, maps or geometric designs with this graph paper.

Draw a Meal PLAN

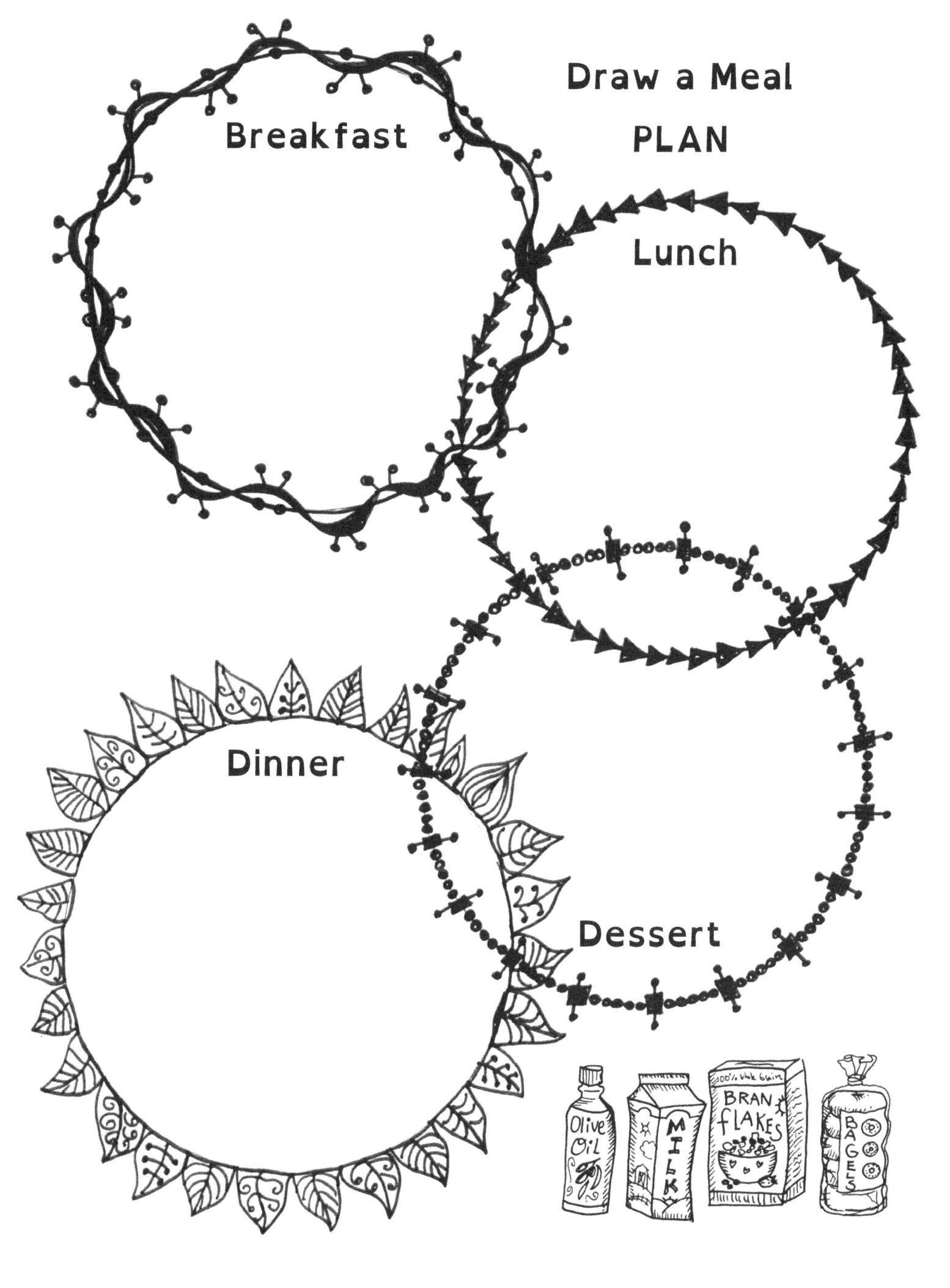

- Breakfast
- Lunch
- Dinner
- Dessert

CHOOSE A DOG BREED:

Where does this breed originally come from?
_____
_____

What are some special traits specific to this breed?
_____
_____

Are there any famous dogs that were this breed?
_____
_____

What else did you find out?
_____
_____

DRAW THE BREED:

DOGS IN HISTORY!
ADD CLIP ART, DRAWINGS, PICTURES OR PHOTOS

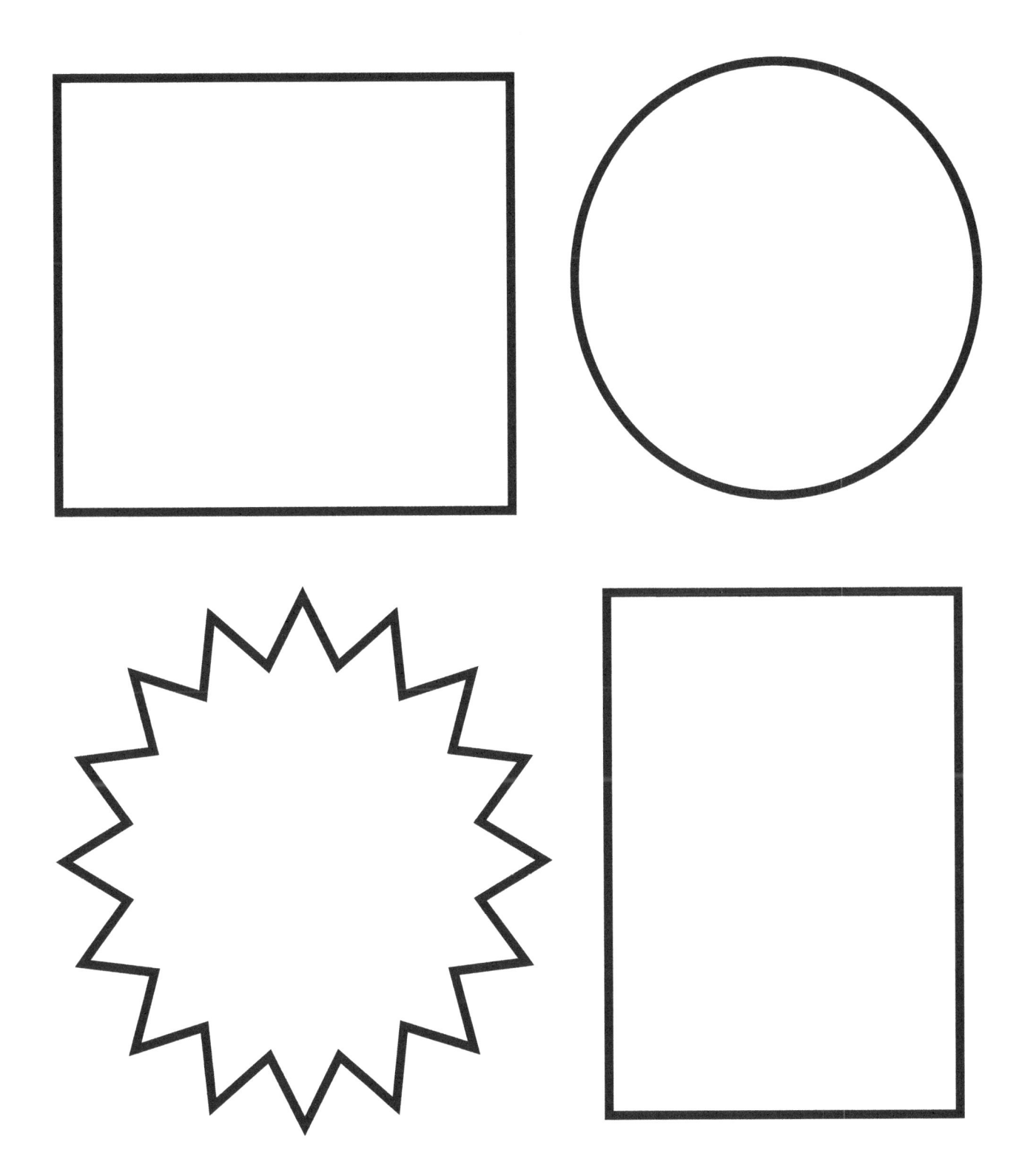

CIRCLE TODAY'S DATE

January
February
March
April
May
June
July
August
September
October
November
December

1 2 3 4 5 6
7 8 9 10 11
12 13 14 15
16 17 18 19
20 21 22 23
24 25 26 27
28 29 30 31

MONDAY
TUESDAY
WEDNESDAY
THURSDAY
FRIDAY
SATURDAY
SUNDAY

2015
2016
2017
2018
2019
2020
2021
2022
2023
2024
2025
2026
2027
2028
2029

Write Today's Date:_____

START YOUR DAY!

Copy a Verse or Quote:

_____
_____
_____
_____
_____
_____
_____

Draw Your Plans

To-Do List

_____
_____
_____
_____
_____
_____
_____

DRAW THE ANSWERS!

WHAT TYPE OF FOOD DO DOGS NEED?

DO THEY EAT ANY OF THE SAME THINGS THAT YOU LIKE TO EAT?

READING TIME - 1 HOUR (SET A TIMER)

Choose Four Books - Read from each book for 15 minutes.

Copy important words or pictures from each book here:

Spelling Time

Find 20 Words with 7 letters each.
Look in your books for words.
Write the words here:

_____   _____

_____   _____

_____   _____

_____   _____

_____   _____

_____   _____

_____   _____

_____   _____

_____   _____

_____   _____

Start Time:
_____

Stop Time:
_____

Screen Time!

Watch a Documentary, Educational Program, Movie, or Tutorial.

TITLE: _____
SUBJECT _____
LOCATION: _____
MESSAGE: _____
_____

Rating:
AWFUL
BAD
LAME
YUCKY
OKAY
NICE
GOOD
GREAT
SUPER
AMAZING

Draw a Scene from the video:

Notes:

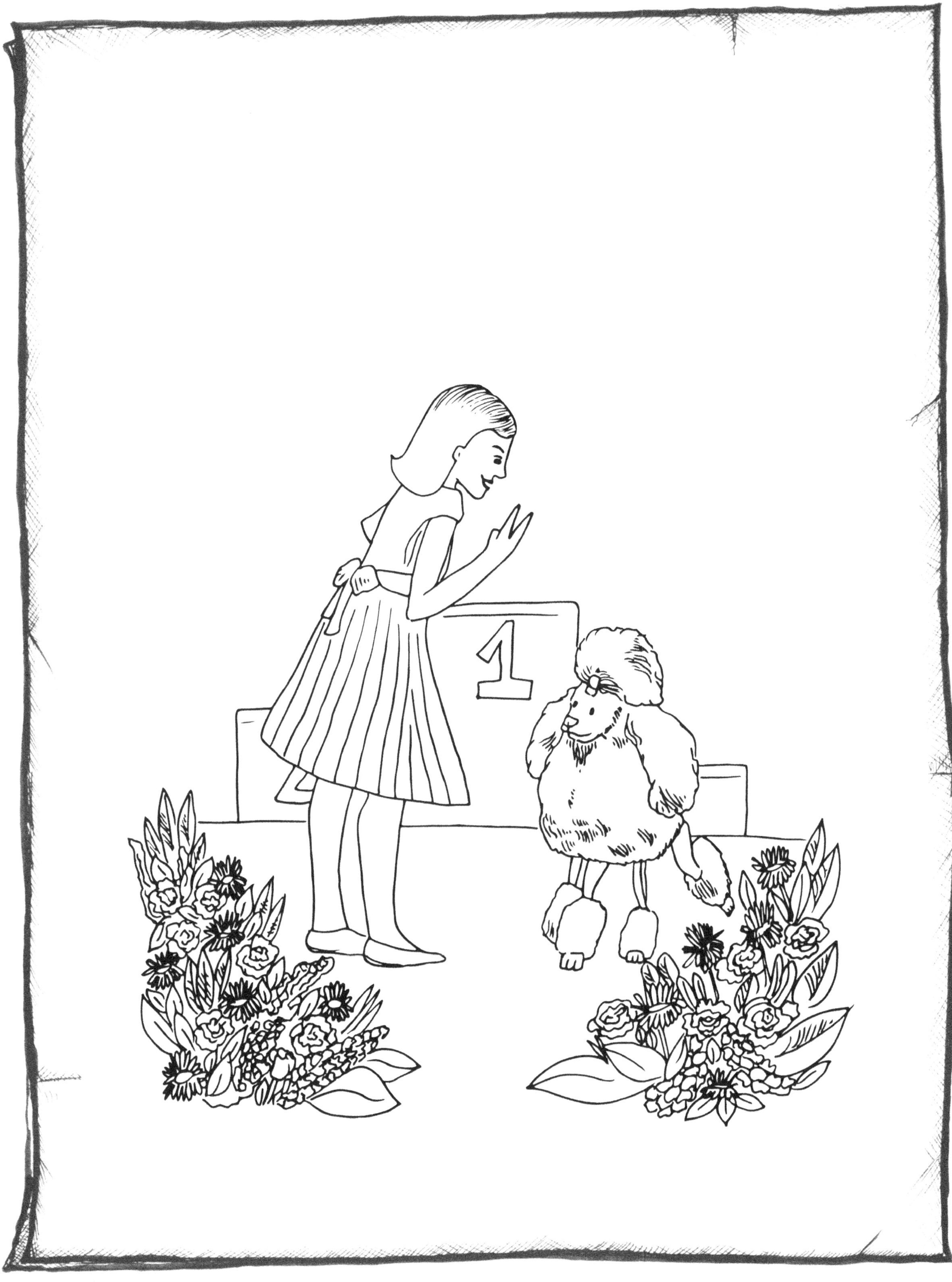
1

CHOOSE A DOG BREED:

_____

Where does this breed originally come from?
_____
_____

What are some special traits specific to this breed?
_____
_____

Are there any famous dogs that were this breed?
_____
_____

What else did you find out?
_____
_____

DRAW THE BREED:

CIRCLE TODAY'S DATE

January
February
March
April
May
June
July
August
September
October
November
December

1 2 3 4 5 6
7 8 9 10 11
12 13 14 15
16 17 18 19
20 21 22 23
24 25 26 27
28 29 30 31

MONDAY
TUESDAY
WEDNESDAY
THURSDAY
FRIDAY
SATURDAY
SUNDAY

2015
2016
2017
2018
2019
2020
2021
2022
2023
2024
2025
2026
2027
2028
2029

Write Today's Date: _____

START YOUR DAY!

Copy a Verse or Quote:

_____
_____
_____
_____
_____
_____

Draw Your Plans

To-Do List

_____
_____
_____
_____
_____

Picture Study

Look closely at this picture.

Think about the lines and shadows.

Practice working with your colored pencils.

Tibetian Mastiff

DRAW THE MISSING PARTS

Use a variety of smooth black drawing pens, with fine points, to complete the picture.

HOW CAN YOU TELL HOW A DOG IS FEELING?

READING TIME - 1 HOUR (SET A TIMER)

Choose Four Books - Read from each book for 15 minutes.

Copy important words or pictures from each book here:

Spelling Time

Find 20 Words with 7 letters each.
Look in your books for words.
Write the words here:

_____   _____

_____   _____

_____   _____

_____   _____

_____   _____

_____   _____

_____   _____

_____   _____

_____   _____

_____   _____

Start Time:
_____

Stop Time:
_____

Screen Time!

Watch a Documentary, Educational Program, Movie, or Tutorial.

TITLE: _____
SUBJECT _____
LOCATION: _____
MESSAGE: _____
_____

Rating:
AWFUL
BAD
LAME
YUCKY
OKAY
NICE
GOOD
GREAT
SUPER
AMAZING

Draw a Scene from the video:

Notes:

TITLE:

COLOR WITH A FRIEND

SHARE THIS PAGE

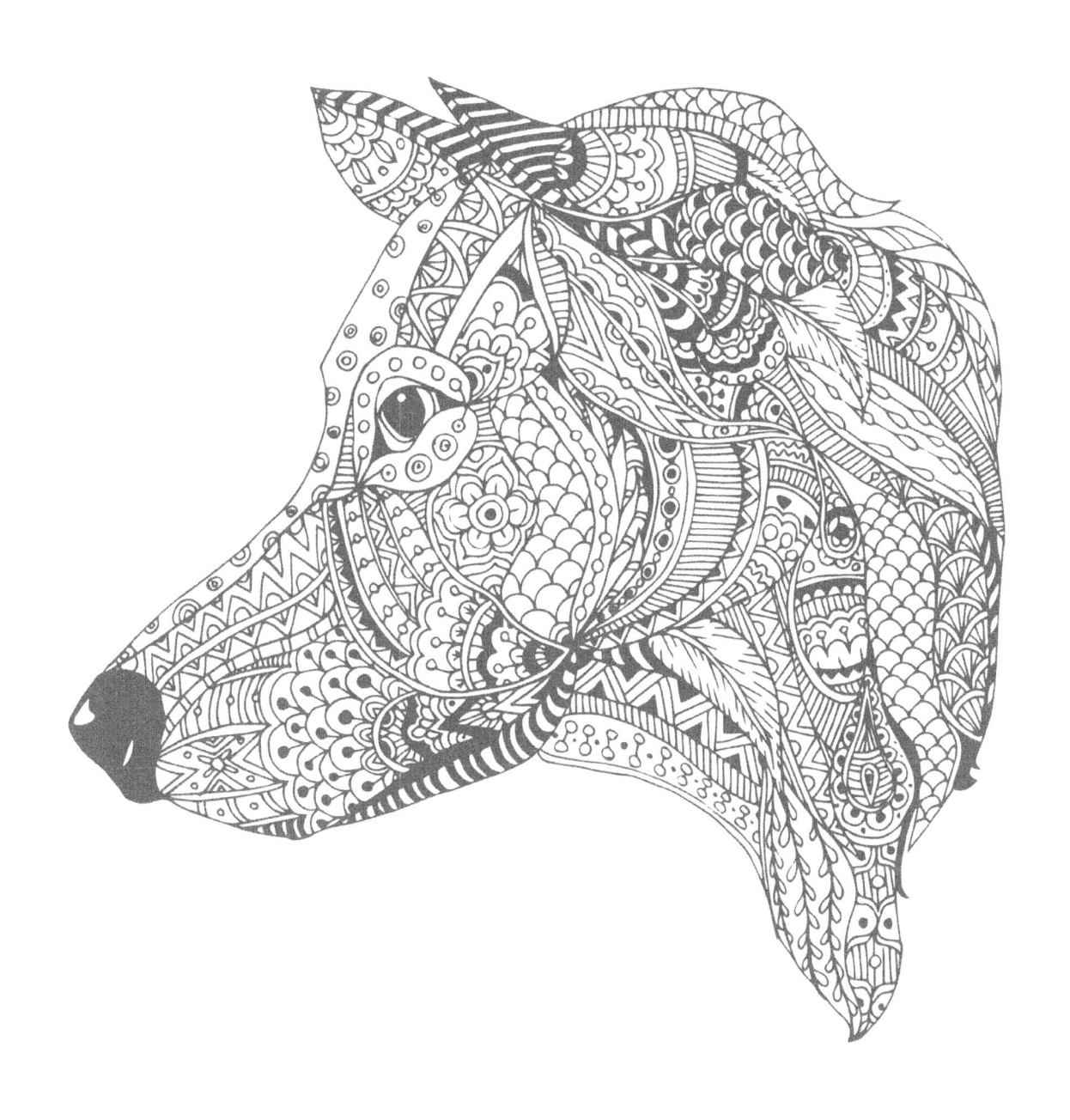

FAMOUS DOGS IN THE HISTORY OF THE WORLD

NAME OF DOG:

TYPE OF DOG:

BEST KNOWN FOR:

DATE OF EVENT:

THE STORY OF THIS INTERESTING DOG:

DOGS IN HISTORY!
ADD CLIP ART, DRAWINGS, PICTURES OR PHOTOS

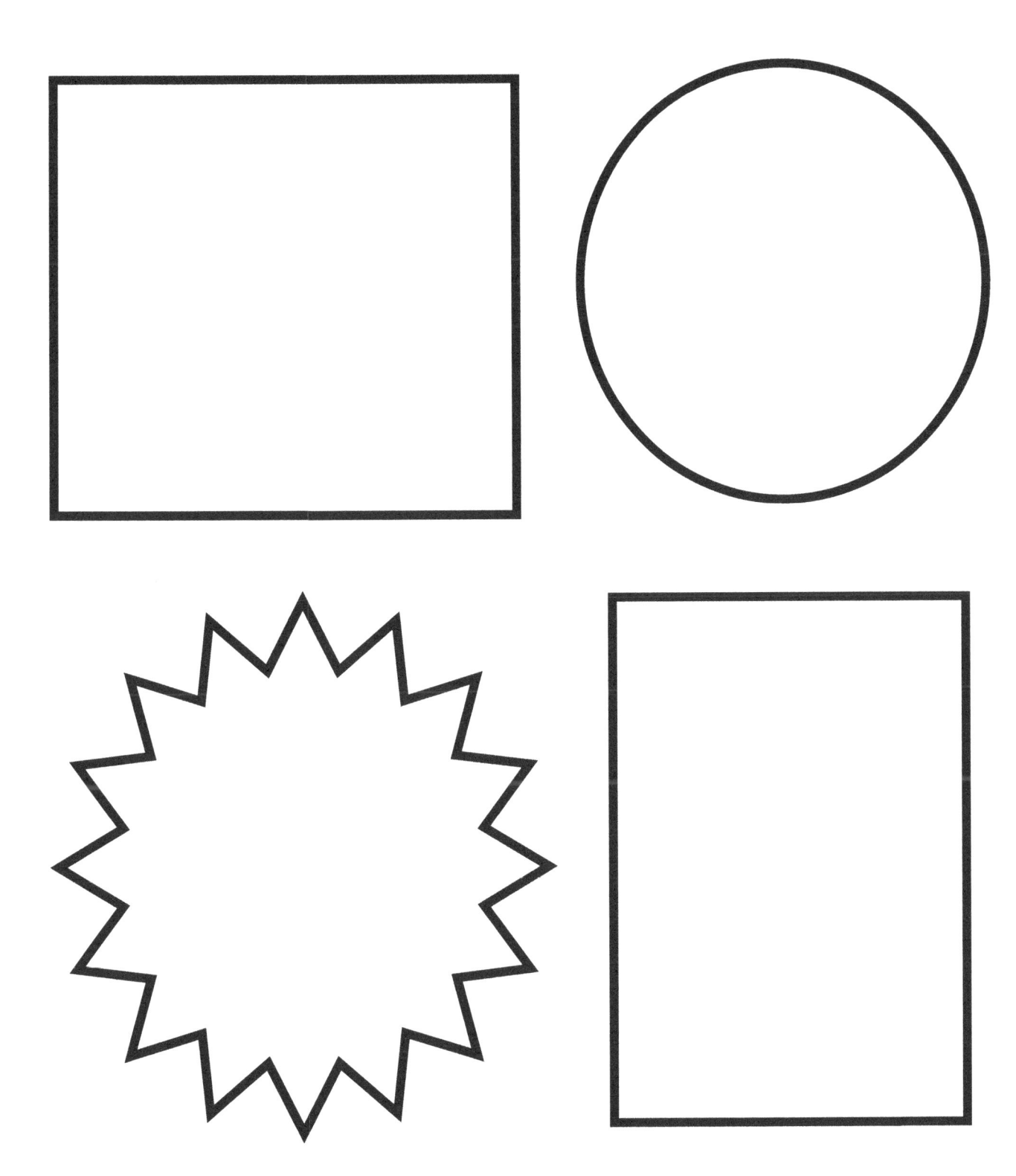

CHOOSE A DOG BREED:

Where does this breed originally come from?
_____
_____

What are some special traits specific to this breed?
_____
_____

Are there any famous dogs that were this breed?
_____
_____

What else did you find out?
_____
_____

DRAW THE BREED:

CAREERS WITH DOGS

LOOK AT THE PICTURE AND TRY TO ANSWER THESE QUESTIONS:

What type of job is this?

_____

What kind of training does a person need to do this job?

_____   _____

What kinds of dogs are involved in this job?

_____

Is there special equipment needed for this job?

_____

How much money does a person earn for doing this job?

_____

Is this a job you would like to do? Why or why not?

_____
_____
_____
_____
_____
_____
_____
_____
_____
_____

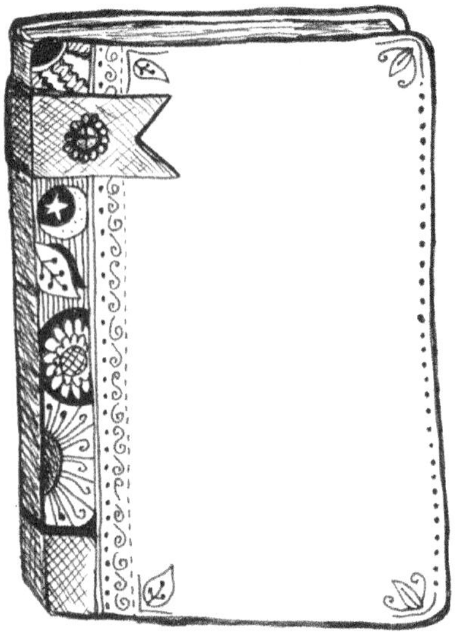
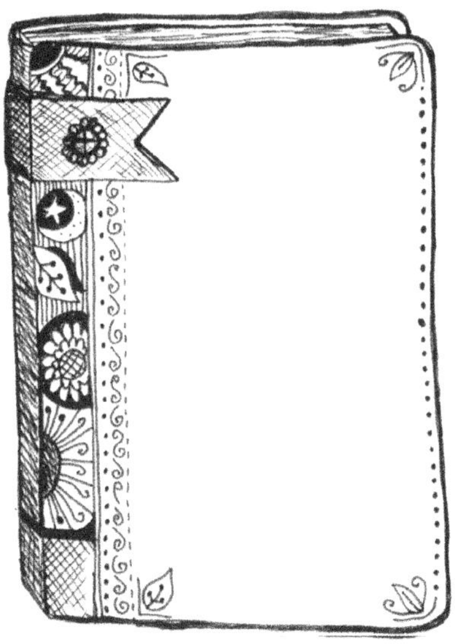
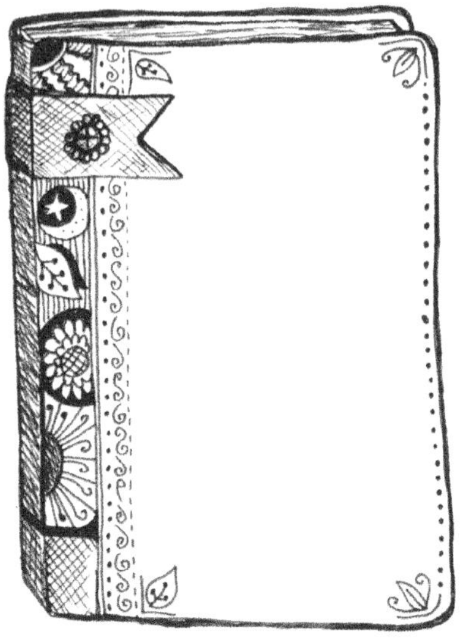
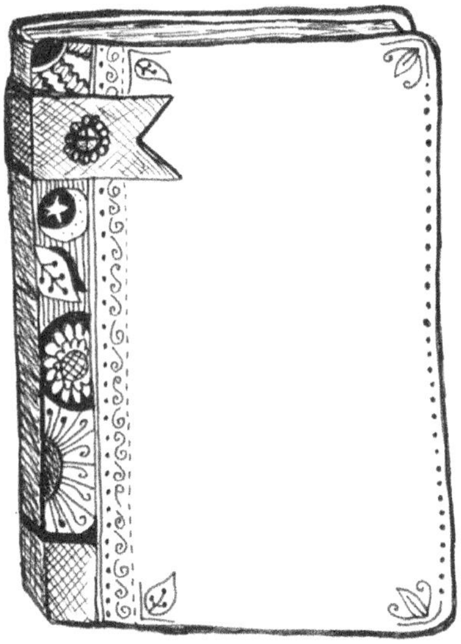
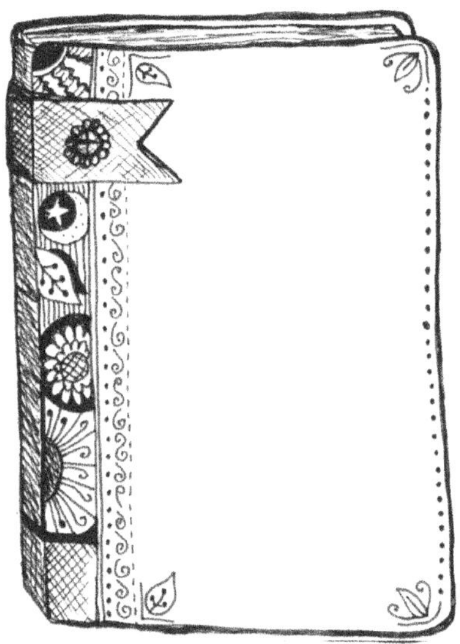
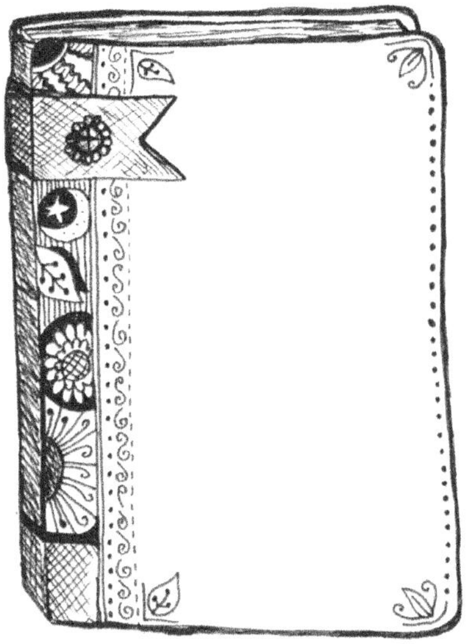
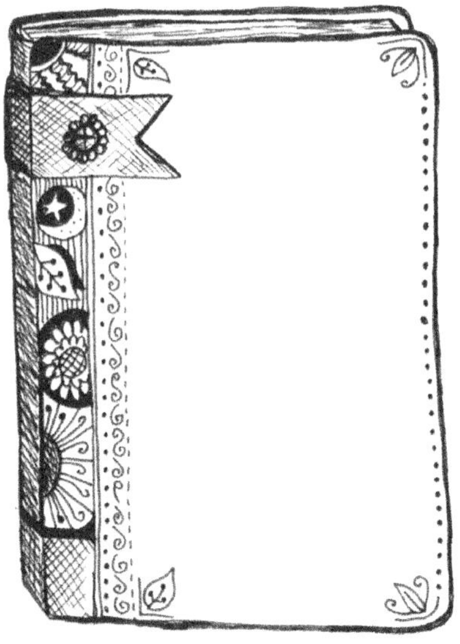
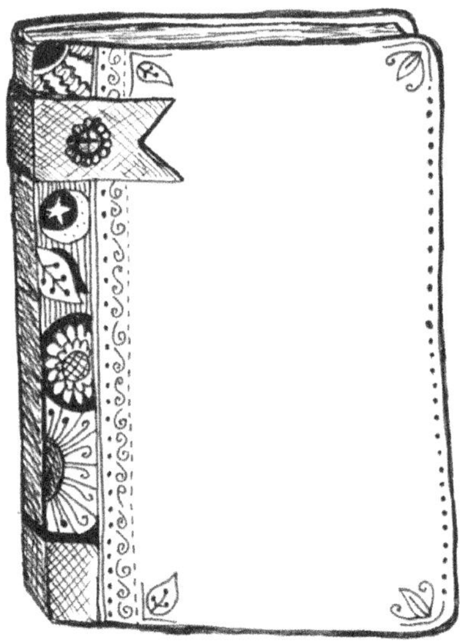
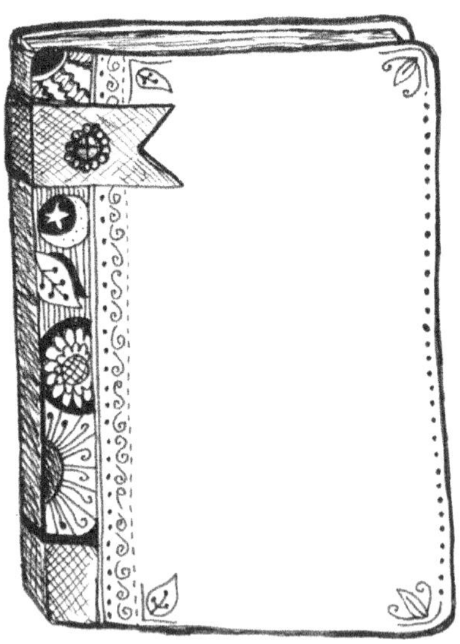

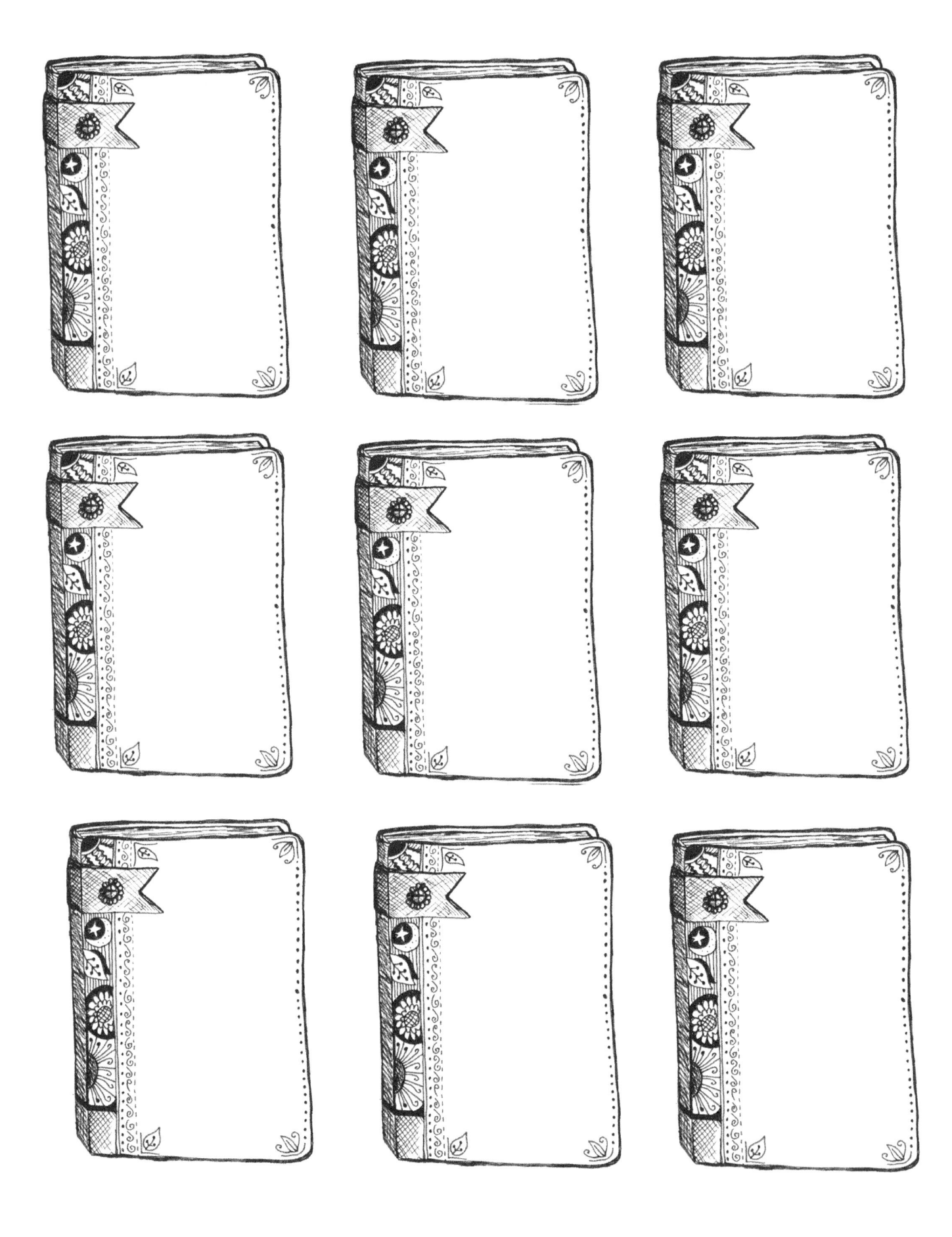

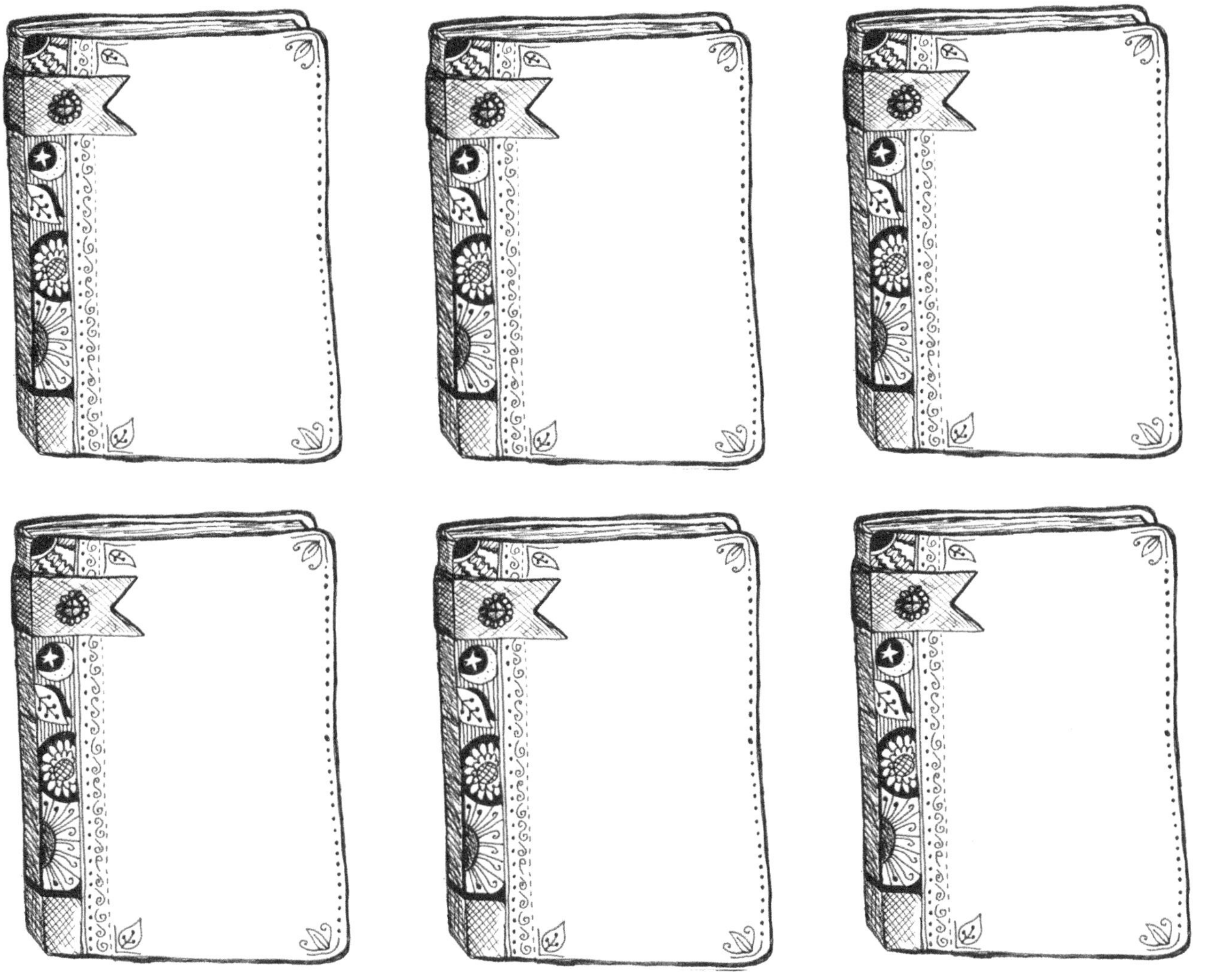

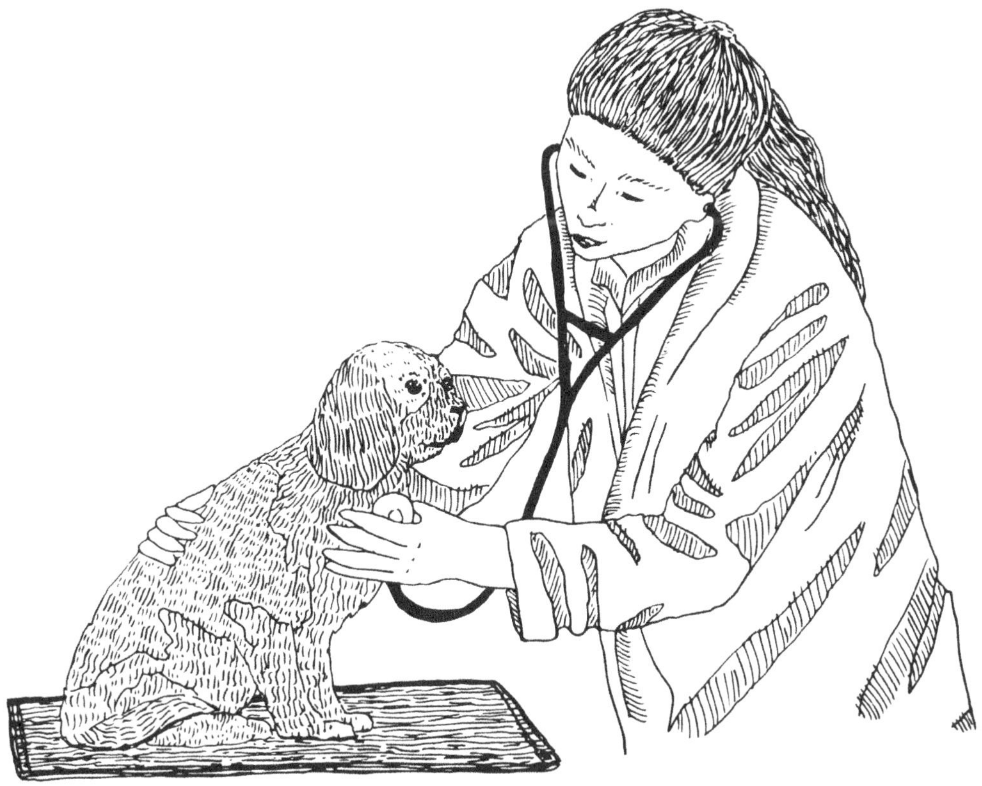

Made in the USA
Columbia, SC
27 August 2019